MARKETING OF HOSPITAL SERVICES

MARKETING OF HOSPITAL SERVICES

By

Dr. C. Eugine Franco
Associate Professor
Deptt. of Commerce
St. Xavier's College
Palayamkottai
Tamil Nadu
&
Dr. X. Antony Thanaraj
Associate Professor
Deptt. of Commerce
Scott Christian College
Nagercoil
Tamil Nadu

DPH

DISCOVERY PUBLISHING HOUSE PVT. LTD.
NEW DELHI-110 002

Published by:
Tilak Wasan
DISCOVERY PUBLISHING HOUSE PVT. LTD.
4831/24, Ansari Road, Prahlad Street
Darya Ganj, New Delhi-110002 (India)
Phone: +91-11-23279245, 43764432
Fax: +91-11-23253475
E-mail: parul.wasan@gmail.com
info@discoverypublishinggroup.com
web: www.discoverypublishinggroup.com

***First Edition:* 2011**
ISBN: 978-81-8356-715-2

Marketing of Hospital Services

Preface

The world is moving fast on its way to becoming service-dominated. The service sector is the fastest growing sector of the Indian economy; it clocked a growth rate of 8 per cent in the 1990s. Professional services like consultancy, nursing, health care, advertising, legal advice, architecture were restrained from actively competing with each other by using the two pillars of promotion viz. advertising and salesmanship. Professional service marketing is becoming a recognised and accepted subset of the marketing discipline. Hospital and health care marketing have only come into its own during the last decade. In the present decade, hospitals have become highly competitive in marketing their services to the public. Hence, this book is on 'Marketing of Professional Services with particular reference to Hospitals'. In this book an exhaustive study has been made as to marketing practices and strategies and other activities connected with the marketing of professional services especially with particular reference to hospitals.

With the ever increasing number of private hospitals poses a severe threat to private profit-making hospitals, inadequacy of both financial and human resources causes serious problems to public sector hospitals. It is also being witnessed that there is an inconsistency in patient turnout at certain health care institutions of both private and public health sectors. It is in this context that this book has been written and published to find out the problems that have been confronted by both the private and government hospitals in providing quality health service to the public, to ascertain the reasons why patients choose and prefer either a private or a government hospitals and also to study the patients' level of attitude towards healthcare services provided by the private as well as the government hospitals in the study area.

Critics are most welcome.

Dr. C. Eugine Franco
Dr. X. Antony Thanaraj

Contents

Abbreviations

AIDS	-	Acquired Immune Deficiency Syndrome
AM	-	Arithmetic Mean
ANOVA	-	Analysis of Variance
ASHA	-	Accredited Social Health Activist
BMSP	-	Basic Minimum Services Programme
BP	-	Blood Pressure
CHC	-	Community Health Centre
CHV	-	Community Health Visitors
CII	-	Confederation of Indian Industry
CSI	-	Church of South India
CSI	-	Core Service Index
DESI	-	Director of Employees State Insurance
DME	-	Director of Medical Education
DMRHS	-	Director of Medical and Rural Health Services
DPH/PM	-	Director of Public Health and Preventive Medicine
FHI	-	Familiarity of the Hospital Index
GDP	-	Gross Domestic Product
HCI	-	Hygienic Condition Index
HI	-	Hospitality Index
HPC	-	Health Sub-Centre
ICU	-	Incentive Care Unit
II	-	Innovativeness Index

IP	-	Inpatient
IT	-	Information Technology
KMO	-	Kaiser Mayer Olkin
LHI	-	Location of the Hospital Index
LMS	-	London Mission Society
MBBS	-	Bachelor of Medicine and Bachelor of Surgery
MD	-	Doctor of Medicine
MNP	-	Minimum Needs Programme
NHRM	-	National Rural Health Mission
P.A	-	Per Annum
P/V Ratio	-	Profit Volume Ratio
PCSI	-	Pre-Consultancy Service Index
PEHSI	-	Physical Evidence of Health Service Index
PHC	-	Primary Health Centre
PSI	-	Peripheral Service Index
QHSI	-	Quality of Hospital Service Index
TBA	-	Trained Birth Attendants
TI	-	Transparency Index
UK	-	United Kingdom
UN	-	United Nations
US	-	United States
USA	-	United States of America
WHO	-	World Health Organization

CHAPTER 1

Introduction and Design of the Study

INTRODUCTION

Every human being possesses the right to life and health, and to the necessities of life, including proper medical services. The 1948 UN Universal Declaration of Human Rights thus proclaims: "*Everyone has the right to a standard of living adequate for the health and well-being of himself and of his family, including food, clothing, housing and medical care and necessary social services, and the right to security in the event of unemployment, sickness, disability, widowhood, old age or other lack of livelihood in circumstances beyond his control. Motherhood and childhood are entitled to special care and assistance*" (Art. 25). And the Preamble to the WHO Constitution states: "*The enjoyment of the highest attainable standard of health is one of the fundamental rights of every human being without distinction of race, religion, politics, economic or social condition*"[1].

Today, the service sector is recognized as a crucial field for economic well-being. Consumption of services is deemed essential today. For example, consumption of services such as education, healthcare, civic services, transport and communication, tourism, entertainment, and sports are considered vital. Event management and media services involving important sports and cultural events keep billions of people spellbound, generate huge revenues, and add dramatically to the economic growth of the countries and states hosting such events. Thus, the consumer focus has shifted largely from more and more consumption of physical goods to greater consumption of services. Indeed, once the basic needs are met, consumers seem to seek more services than goods, and a higher standard of living usually means increased consumption of services rather than higher consumption of goods only[2].

The world is moving fast on its way to becoming service-dominated. In the last century, different sectors had shown their dominance. The first era belonged to agriculture. This was followed by the supremacy of manufacturing or the growth of industries. By the end of the twentieth century, most of the developed and developing nations became service-based[3]. There are a number of studies which provide strong evidence to the fact that the service sector has been growing faster than the commodity producing sectors in most of the developing economies[4]. The service sector is the fastest growing sector of the Indian economy, it clocked a growth rate of 8 per cent in the 1990s. One in every two Indians earns his/her living from the service sector. This is a very diversified sector ranging from housemaids to neurosurgeons.

The health care industry in India has come a long way from the days when only those who could afford it had to travel abroad. Today patients from the neighbuoring countries, the Middle East, the UK and even the USA are flocking to India for specialised and quality treatment at lower costs. India receives more than 1,50,000 medical tourists every year[5]. The private sector provides more than 80 per cent of health services in India[6].

Marketing of Professional Services

Professional services like consultancy, nursing, healthcare, advertising, legal advice, architecture were restrained from actively competing with each other by using media like advertising and salesmanship. Also, these firms did not visualise the importance of marketing know-how in the conduct of their business due to lack of awareness about the relevance of marketing in services. Marketing was something that has been too much associated with fast moving goods sector. Now things seem to be changing. Various professional bodies adopt a more liberal posture. They are becoming more open about using marketing as a business philosophy. Private hospitals, lawyers, management consultants and educational institutions are beginning to use marketing, albeit not in an integrated manner.

Service marketers responded to environmental forces and began to work across disciplines and with academicians and business practitioners from around the world to develop and document marketing practices for service industries.[7] Professional service marketing is becoming a recognised and accepted subset of the marketing discipline. Professional marketing aims at stating long range marketing objectives and strategies in the areas of business growth and profitability.

Need for Marketing of Professional Services

There has been phenomenal growth of professional services in the recent years. More people are employed in professional service industries than in manufacturing industries. There is a fast development and growth, of the 'Service Economy', first in North America and Western Europe and now in Asia. It is reasonable to assume that the decline of traditional manufacturing industries, and the increasing use of micro-technology, will mean a continued shift towards employment in, and expansion of, this service sector of economics in developed countries[8].

The increasingly competitive service markets of today, however, are leading to a change in attitude towards marketing. Professionals have turned to marketing to help them cope with a rapidly changing and difficult to understand environment, increasing competition and greater public dissatisfaction[9]. Hence, professionals now-a-days take marketing seriously and seek to become more professional in their marketing efforts.

Professional service firms have, as compared to other types of firms, an obstacle to efficient marketing; in some professional groups, marketing is actively resisted: it is looked down upon and considered below the dignity of the professional firms.[10]

Hospital Service Marketing

Hospital and healthcare marketing have only come into its own during the last decade. However, it is important to remember that marketing is used in public health campaigns throughout history. The communication techniques used to educate population about prevention and treatment procedures for different epidemics and communicable diseases are the beginning of the concept of health care marketing. In fact, health education through Government health departments is the foundation of health care marketing.

It is also important to remember that marketing has been used extensively by public health departments, pharmaceutical firms, medical supply businesses and health maintenance organisations during the last few decades. In a far cry from the earlier scenario when hospitals viewed their services as essential (therefore bringing in the patients any way), today healthcare institutions fall over each other to draw in the patient, primarily using the quality platform to position themselves. One client segment that practically all healthcare institutions are concentrating on is corporate houses — perceived as the fastest emerging breed of the rich and famous. Under such circumstances, the focus has shifted from the curative to the preventive aspect of healthcare.[11]

In the late 1970s the U.S. Supreme Court struck down many of the bans against advertising, holding that they effectively reduce competition by depriving organisations and individuals of the right to inform potential patients of information about the services and depriving potential patients of receiving that information. Many professions responded to the ruling with comprehensive advertising campaigns.[12]

In India, though the code of ethics restricts professionals from advertising campaigns, hospitals have slowly started making campaigns in the early 1990s in order to cope with the competition and other environmental changes.

In the present decade, hospitals have become highly competitive in marketing their services to the public. It has become common to see hospitals advertising their services via a number of media. Hence, this study is undertaken to know the various marketing practices and strategies and other activities connected with the marketing of professional services especially with particular reference to hospitals.

STATEMENT OF THE PROBLEM

Adam Smith, the Father of Economics, says that *"Nothing happens until somebody sells something"*. Further, Robert Louis Stevenson, an eminent marketing expert says that *"everybody lives by selling something"*[13]. Thus, it is true that anything and everything has to be sold out at a profit to the seller and at a benefit to the buyer. Since selling is an integral part of marketing, we can say that everything is marketing and exchange has been considered as the heart of marketing.

By hospital marketing or marketing healthcare services, we mean making available the healthcare or medicare services to the different categories of users in such a way that they get quality health services, at a reasonable fee structure, on the right time and in a decent way[14]. Thus, hospitality becomes an essential part of hospital marketing and it is in this context that we find hospital marketing or marketing of healthcare services as a managerial process that helps a professional in formulating a sound marketing mix in tune with the fluctuating intensity of health problems and in accordance with the fluctuating demand of patients.

During the yester decades, marketing focussed on profit generation and during the yester years, marketing concentrated on customer satisfaction; marketing now emphasises on social well being. This makes it clear that the philosophy of marketing is related and important not only in the case of profit-making organisations but also in the case of non-profit-making organisations. And as such, marketing is highly useful not only for private hospitals, but also for Government hospitals. As marketing has become an important instrument in increasing both the efficacy and efficiency of an organisation, it is of paramount importance for the effective delivery of health services, both by the private health sector and the public health sector as well. Hospitals of both sorts are expected to render healthcare services of preventive and curative measures. And, in rendering both preventive and curative health services, hospitals must be in a position to blend all the 7 Ps of service marketing namely product, price, place, promotion, people, physical evidences and process appropriately and judiciously.

Eventually, the marketing of professional services in general and hospital marketing in particular becomes different in many aspects and respects compared to goods marketing. Major transformations which occur both in the internal and external environments of healthcare organisations necessitated professional organisations including hospitals to follow marketing principles and practices. A more number of professionals supplied, increased complex behaviour of patients, persistent technological changes and developments, increased competition, availability of alternative medicines, new code of conduct imposed by professional bodies and increased difficulties in defining service quality and also in providing promised quality service demanded medical professionals to develop a sustainable marketing strategy for hospitals.

While the ever increasing number of private hospitals poses a severe threat to private profit-making hospitals, inadequacy of both financial and human resources causes serious problems to public sector hospitals. It is also being witnessed that there is an inconsistency in patient turnout at certain healthcare institutions of both private and public health sectors. It is in this context that this study has been undertaken, to find out the problems that have been confronted by both the private and Government hospitals in providing quality health service to the public, to assess the cost of private hospital services and analyse the cost and return of private health service providers, to ascertain the reasons why patients choose and prefer either a private or a Government hospital and also to study the patients' level of attitude towards healthcare services provided by the private as well as the Government hospitals in the study area.

THE REVIEW OF THE PREVIOUS STUDIES

In advanced countries like the U.S.A and Britain, marketing of professional services particularly hospital services gained momentum around three decades ago and hence there are many studies in this area. In India, hospital service marketing is in its infancy stage and hence there is no as much literature as found in advanced countries in this area. Since there is no such similar study done previously in the selected area, some of the available literatures from foreign studies are brought to light.

Foreign Studies

Philip Kotler and Richard A. Connor, (1977) attempted a study on "Marketing Professional Services". The study was undertaken to explicate the role of marketing in professional services firms. The conclusion drawn by this study is responding to the question facing professional firms i.e. whether to involve in marketing or not. In their field of marketing, the question is how to do it effectively. As the firm's competitors resorted increasingly to installing an organised programme for business development, the professional firms could no longer remain indifferent to the discipline of marketing.[15]

William J. Winston (U.S.A) made a study on "The Evolution of Hospital Marketing" (1986) According to him the evolution of the marketing concept was through health education by the public sector health departments.[16]

Quality of hospital service: A study comparing 'Asian' and 'non-Asian' patients in Middlesbrough was carried out by Rajan Madhok. Bhopal to compare 'Asian' and 'non-Asian patients' experience and their satisfaction with non-clinical aspects of their hospital care, and to evaluate and effect subsequent provision of 'Asian' food. The study revealed that 47 (90 per cent) 'Asians' and 14 (27 per cent) 'non-Asians' required a special diet but 19 per cent and 86 per cent respectively, received it; and 'Asians' were less satisfied with the food overall. Despite being at a disadvantage 'Asian' patients seldom complained. Equitable health care provision for ethnic minorities requires a level of service comparable with that enjoyed by the majority community[17].

A study titled "Patient loyalty versus satisfaction: Implications for Quality and Marketing Strategies" was carried out by Baba Wazzan, (2000). This mixed-method study of three competing hospitals in Lebanon differentiates among the organizational factors for healthcare delivery that affect the intention to return and the amount of satisfaction, and also measures their respective impacts. The study also examined these relationships across different department specialties. The findings demonstrate that factors that increase patient satisfaction differed from those that influence a patient's intention to return, which in turn differed from those that influence a patient's decision to come back or to direct to another hospital.[18]

A study on Consumer Expectation Formation in Health Care Services: A psycho-social model conducted by Russ, Kenneth Randall (2006). A psycho-social model of consumer expectation formation in a healthcare service context was developed and tested. The research identified that the uncertainty of a health service encounter may cause certain consumer segments to choose coping strategies and expectation processes based on their locus of control orientation from along a continuum ranging from "approach-active" to "avoidance-positive". High internal locus of control was associated with greater amounts of internal search, the formation of more accurate process expectations and also higher service quality expectations. The linkage of external locus of control to social support was not supported. However, social support was associated with higher levels of bolstering — an effect based coping strategy in which consumers minimize the risks of a chosen alternative and maximize the risks of non-chosen health service alternative. Seventy per cent of the variance in the model was explained by the structural model. The model provides a useful basis for segmentation in healthcare services to improve consumer satisfaction based on designing integrated marketing communications and service offering which meet unique psycho-social needs and consumer expectations.[19]

An exploratory study on 'Measuring and Explaining the Managerial Efficiency of Private Medical Clinics in Bangladesh' by Rahman, Mohammed, A. (2006). The study found that there is considerable inefficiency in the way medical clinics in the private sector currently operate. The study determined that as much as 1,146 beds, 406 doctors, 600 nurses and 2,475 staff could be reduced if all the clinics operated at the 'best practice' level. In contrast, an additional 14,386 outpatients, 2,844 surgical patients and 6,404 gynaecological patients could be treated with existing resources.[20]

Indian Studies

A study titled "An Examination of Public and Private Sector Sources of Inpatient Care in Trivandrum District, Kerala (India)", was carried out by Rick K Homan and K R Thankappan, (1999). Based on a 5 point Likert type scale of self-reported satisfaction, patients from the public sector reported lower levels of satisfaction with the care received than the level of satisfaction of the patients from the private sector facilities. The study suggests that the demand for hospital care among private sector patients may be fairly inelastic. The hidden cost of care associated with care in public hospitals was unaffordable for the poor.[21]

A study titled "characteristics and Structure of Private Hospital Sector in Urban India: A Study of Madras City" was attempted by Muraleedharan VR. to analyze the size and geographical distribution of the private hospitals in Madras city. The study found out that the private hospital sector in india has grown passively over the years, without any kind of state policy directing its growth and development. as a result, the private hospitals have had no incentives to follow any norms either with regard to physical infrastructures (space per bed, provision of certain utilities such as drinking water, drainage facilities, elevators, back-up power etc) or with regard to the staffing pattern. For example, there are no common norms for setting up an intensive care unit. As a result there is a vast variation in provision of ICU facilities across private hospitals. The study has shown that in a number of accounts there is prima facie evidence for policy makers to worry about the quality and the quantum of physical infrastructure available for good patient care in private hospitals.[22]

A study titled "Characteristics of Private Medical Practice in India: A Provider Perspective" by Bhat Ramesh (1999) was undertaken to identify areas of intervention so that the private health sector becomes responsive to the problems of its growth and also to understand the views of each stakeholder. The study found out that 45 per cent of the doctors spend less than 15 minutes on each patient so that they are able to see more patients. Fifty per cent of the private doctors occasionally referred patients to other specialists. In case of investigations, 56 per cent of doctors referred patients frequently to diagnostic facilities. The study indicated that recommendations by physicians are generally based on quality and proximity factors. The fee setting practices of providers are primarily determined by cost considerations (47 per cent). There is very little influence of professional medical bodies on deciding the fees charged by providers. Only 11 per cent of the providers decide on fee on the basis of association's recommendations. Only 59 per cent of the providers indicated that patients ask for a copy of the prescription and diagnosis. About 90 per cent of the providers indicate that private practice has become capital intensive. The survey results indicate that 46 per cent of the providers do not depend upon borrowed finance for their total capital employed. In these cases, all investments are financed by the owner(s). On the other hand, 35 per cent of the providers get involved in heavy debt to finance their investments. Only about 19 per cent of the providers depend upon moderate levels of debt to finance their capital investments.[23]

A study on 'determinants of access to and utilization of health care services in Kerala' was carried out by Shenoy kt (1999) to study the utilization pattern and factors determining the utilization of private and public healthcare services, and also the patterns of expenditure. The lower socio-economic groups were significantly less likely to use private services than higher se groups. The urban subjects were significantly less likely to use private services than rural subjects. Patients with chronic illnesses were significantly less likely to use private services compared to those with acute illnesses. Patients who travelled long distances (more than 5-km) were significantly less likely to use private services compared to those who travelled a less distance. Private services are more utilized than the public services. Strategies to improve public health care services need to be planned for better access and utilization.[24]

A study titled "Management of Healthcare Service Sector — A Study on Primary Health Centres" by Singh and Sunaina, examine the management of healthcare services in primary health centres in rural areas. The study revealed that the preference for primary health centre is mainly by the poor community because of its instability to afford secondary and tertiary hospitals. Many of the respondents prefer primary health centres only for minor ailments. Many of the patients are not cured inspite of taking treatment from primary health centres and under a strained economic condition they are forced to opt for private hospitals for getting better treatment.[25]

A study was taken up on "behaviour of the private sector in the health services market of Bombay" by Yesudian C.A.K. to study the complex behaviour of health service providers in the private sector in terms of different forms of operation, delivery of services, and to assess the existing control mechanisms and policy options available for their regulation. According to the respondents, wastes such as surgical material, bandages, dressing materials and placenta, were usually thrown in the public dustbins. Almost all the respondents felt that the nursing homes did not have professionally trained staff. All the respondents agreed that the patient care would suffer badly if qualified nurses were not employed. The respondents also emphasized the dangers of the administration of wrong drugs by the untrained nurses. They were highly critical of the private clinics and nursing homes because such clinics employed uneducated staff.[26]

THE REVIEW OF THE RELEVANT CONCEPTS OF COSTS AND RETURNS

The review of the relevant concepts in determining the cost and return analysis of private health service providers has been organised under the following two heads:

(*i*) Cost structure

(*ii*) Returns

Cost Structure: The right decision on investment in hospital activities can be taken only when valuable information on costs and returns are available. Such information will be very useful to improve servicing pattern as well as efficiency through the least cost combination of resources.

Mittal and Sexena defined fixed costs in service sectors as those which were independent of the level of production whereas the variable costs vary with the level of output[27].

Mohan classified costs as direct cost and indirect costs. According to him indirect costs consist of annual share of establishment cost, interest on fixed and working capital and depreciation on fixed assets. Direct costs include operation costs and other direct charges.[28] In the present study, the total cost of production is classified into fixed costs and variable costs.

Measurement of Variables

Rental Value of Land : The Directorate of Economics and Statistics imputed rental value for owned land at the existing rate of rent prevailing for similar land in the location. In the case of leased land, the actual rent paid was taken.[29] In the present study, all the sample providers owned the lands where their hospitals have been built up. Therefore the rental value prevailing in the adjoining areas was taken as the rental value of hospital area under study.

Depreciation : Depreciation was charged to meet the loss due to wear and tear on fixed assets. Here depreciation was calculated under straight-line method. It was done separately for hospital building, machinery, tools, equipment and furniture. Depreciation was charged at the rate specified below.[30]

Hospital Building	-	2 per cent
Machinery	-	10 per cent
Tools and equipment	-	25 per cent
Furniture	-	10 per cent

SCOPE OF THE STUDY

The scope of the study is confined to the marketing aspects of both the private and the Government hospitals located in Kanyakumari district. Over the years, Kanyakumari district has built-up a vast health-infrastructure and manpower at primary, secondary and tertiary care in the Government and the private sectors. The district has a good network of Government hospitals, primary health centres and health sub-centres, providing advanced methods of treatment to the people. Private health care services in Kanyakumari district have grown and got diversified during the last two decades. These consist of a range of players who provide services in both rural and urban areas. As regards Government hospitals, the study includes Governmental hospitals including Primary Health Centres (PHCs) and Health Sub-Centres (HSCs) of the district. As regards private hospitals, only the private hospitals, nursing homes and clinics by private parties that are run for profit-making have been included in the study. Again, in the case of private hospitals, only hospitals, nursing homes and clinics with sole proprietorship have been chosen, for the single reason that these types of private health sector establishments are found in plenty in the district. Further, the study is confined to the above-mentioned private and Government hospitals providing only advanced medicinal treatment — that is allopathic health service in the four areas namely maternity, paediatric, orthopaedic and general medicine. Further, as regards patients, the study is confined to the inpatients of both the Government and the private hospitals.

OBJECTIVES OF THE STUDY

The present study has been undertaken with the following objectives:

1. To study the profile of health services provided in Kanyakumari district.
2. To assess the socio-economic conditions of the patient respondents in the study area.
3. To analyse the decision-making factors in the marketing of healthcare services.
4. To assess the attitude of the patients towards the marketing of hospital services.
5. To assess the cost of hospital services and to analyse the cost and return of the private healthcare service providers.
6. To assess and analyse the problems faced by the providers of hospital services and the patients respondents and also to offer suitable suggestion to overcome the problems.

HYPOTHESES

Based on the objectives of the study, the following hypotheses were framed:

1. There exists no significant relationship between the literacy level and the level of attitude of the patient respondents towards the services rendered by the hospitals.
2. There exists no significant relationship between the occupation and the level of attitude of the patient respondents towards the services rendered by the hospitals.
3. There exists no significant relationship between the marital status and the level of attitude of the patient respondents towards the services rendered by the hospitals.
4. There exists no significant relationship between the family income and the level of attitude of the patient respondents towards the services rendered by the hospitals.
5. There exists no significant relationship between the number of members in the family and the level of attitude of the patient respondents towards the services rendered by the hospitals.
6. There exists no significant relationship between the area of residence and the level of attitude of the patient respondents towards the services rendered by the hospitals.
7. There exists no significant relationship between the age group and the level of attitude of the patient respondents towards the services rendered by the hospitals.
8. There exists no significant relationship between the gender and the level of attitude of the patient respondents towards the services rendered by the hospitals.

OPERATIONAL DEFINITION OF CONCEPTS

Allopathy (Greek) : Allos - other; pathos - suffering, a term invented by Hahnemann, the promulgator of homoeopathy, to describe that method of treatment of diseases that consists of using medicines whose action upon the body in health produces morbid phenomena different from those of the disease treated.

Ayurveda : Ayurvedic medicine is an ancient system of health care that is native to the Indian subcontinent. Ayurveda is also one among the few traditional systems of medicine to contain a sophisticated system of surgery.

Client : One for whom professional medical services are rendered. In other words a customer or a patient.

Consultant : A person who gives expert or professional medical advice.

Core service : The most important part of hospital services or the main services.

Cost : It refers to the total expense which is incurred in providing health service.

Data : Known or granted information from which a conclusion can be drawn.

Doctor : In common parlance a "doctor" means a physician, or quite generally a qualified medical practitioner, whether he has taken the degree of doctor of medicine, M.D or not.

Fee : A payment for availing professional medical service.

Homoeopathy : It is a treatment that seeks to stimulate the body's defence mechanisms and processes so as to prevent or treat illnesses.

Hospital : An institution for the temporary reception of the sick. An organisation where patients get medical advice / treatment for curing their illnesses or ailments.

Hospitality : It is the art of making people/patients feel at home.

Market : A market is the set of actual and potential patients for an offer of medical advice / treatment.

Marketing : Marketing is the analysis, planning, implementation, and control of carefully formulated programmes designed to bring about voluntary exchanges of values with target markets for the purpose of achieving organisational objectives.

Marketing Mix : Marketing mix is the particular blend of controllable marketing variables the firm uses to achieve its objective in the target market.

Market Segmentation : Market segmentation is the act of dividing a total heterogeneous market into distinct, meaningful and smaller group of consumers who have similar characteristic features.

Medical Tourism : Medical tourism refers to travel undergone for the purpose of medical treatment and rejuvenation.

Patients : Patients are those who avail healthcare services from hospitals, they are the ultimate users of hospital services.

Peripheral Services : Peripheral services are the additional services like accommodation for the attendants, safe drinking water, pay-phone services and the like which are offered by the hospitals to make their services distinct to others.

Potential Market : The potential market is the set of consumers who profess some level of interest in a defined market offer.

Physical Evidences : The physical evidence of a service is a tangible clue, which creates an impression about the service. In the case of a hospital, examples of physical evidences are: the building exteriors, parking, waiting areas, medical equipment and the patient care rooms.

Primary Care : Primary care covers a broad range of health and preventive services, including health education, counselling, disease prevention and screening.

Product : A product is anything that can be offered to a market to satisfy a need. It includes physical objects, services, persons, places, organisations and ideas.

Professional Services : Professional services tend to be labour intensive but they provide highly customised services like physicians, lawyers, accountants and architects.

Provider : A provider is the one who provides medical services either by owning a hospital or by serving in a Government hospital.

Returns : It refers to the total revenue generated by providing health service minus the total cost involved in it.

Satisfaction : Satisfaction is a state of mind felt by a patient who has experienced a medical performance (or outcome) that has fulfilled his or her expectations.

Service : A service is any activity or benefit that one party can offer to another that is essentially intangible and does not result in the ownership of anything.

Secondary Care : The term secondary care is a service provided by medical specialists who generally do not have first contact with patients, for example cardiologists, urologists and dermatologists.

Siddha : Siddha system is one of the oldest systems of medicine in India. The Siddha system is largely therapeutic in nature.

Tertiary Care : In medicine, tertiary healthcare is a specialised consultative care, usually on referral from primary or secondary medical care personnel.

Unani : In India, Unani practitioners are allowed to practice as qualified doctors, as the Indian Government approves their practice. Most medicines and remedies (often called herbs and foods) used in Unani are also used in Ayurveda.

GEOGRAPHICAL AREA COVERED

For the purpose of the study Kanyakumari, the southern most district of India, has been selected for this study since it has contributed much to the field of Medicine. Over the years, Kanyakumari district has built up a vast health infrastructure and manpower at the primary, secondary and tertiary care in both public as well as private health sectors. Over the past few years, medical tourism has gained momentum in South India and significantly in Kanyakumari district. Further, the very fact that the researcher hails from this district is an added advantage. All these aspects necessitated the researcher to select the geographical area of Kanyakumari district as a whole which is otherwise bifurcated into two revenue divisions — situated in Nagercoil and Padmanabhapuram.

PERIOD OF THE STUDY

The required primary data have been collected both from the patient respondents of the private and the Government hospitals and also from the providers of both the private and the public health services. The survey was conducted during seven months from December 2007 to June 2008. Further, primary data collected concerning the costs and returns of hospital services from the providers of private health service are related to the year 2007-2008.

METHODOLOGY

The study pertains to the marketing of hospitals in Kanyakumari district. Both public and private healthcare sectors have been selected for this purpose. However, private hospitals run by charitable institutions, trusts and non-Governmental organisations are not taken for the study. Both the Government and the private hospitals have been classified into four categories, namely maternity, paediatric, orthopaedic and General medicine hospitals. Hence, this study has been confined to both the Government and the private hospitals of Kanyakumari district providing only the above-mentioned four categories of health services. The study is exploratory in character and therefore the 'survey method' has been adopted.

Both the primary and the secondary data have been used to study the objectives of this research. From the perspective of the providers of healthcare, the problems that have been confronted by them in providing health services have been duly considered and from the perspective of the providers of private healthcare, the cost and return analysis has been drawn. From the patients' perspective, their reasons for preferring either the Government or the private hospitals, their level of attitude towards the health services provided by both the Government and the private hospitals and the problems that have been faced by them in availing health services both from the Government and the private hospitals have been elicited. Hence, two separate interview schedules have been structured and used as tools to collect information from providers and patients.

SAMPLING DESIGN

The survey is conducted only on the target population of the four categories of hospitals / health services as specified earlier. For the purpose of taking a sample, the details regarding the four categories of Government hospitals were obtained from the Deputy Director of Health services, Nagercoil and the details regarding the four categories of private hospitals were obtained from Indian Medical Association, Nagercoil, Marthandam and Kanyakumari. There are 310 public sector health establishments namely Government hospitals, Primary Health Centres (PHCs) and Health Sub-Centres (HSCs) in the district, and 295 private sector health establishments namely private hospitals, nursing homes and clinics are found in the district. With regard to the selection of sample hospitals, stratified random sampling was adopted.

With regard to the selection of sample patients, of the total 310 Government hospitals in the district, 50 hospitals (20 Maternity and Paediatric and 30 Orthopaedic and General medicine) have been selected by using stratified random sampling technique. Four patients from each such sample hospital have been selected using convenience sampling technique. Thus, the sample size of the patients of Government hospitals amounts to 200 (80 from Maternity and Paediatric + 120 from Orthopaedic and General medicine). Likewise, of the 295 private hospitals in the district, 50 hospitals (20 Maternity and Paediatric and 30 Orthopaedic and General medicine) have been selected by using stratified random sampling technique. Four patients from each such sample hospital have been selected using convenience sampling technique. Thus, the sample size of the patients of the private hospitals amounts to 200 (80 from Maternity and Paediatric + 120 from Orthopaedic and General medicine). Thus, the total size of the sample patients is 400.

TOOLS FOR COLLECTION OF DATA

Two separate interview schedules were structured by the researcher in order to elicit relevant information from the provider of health service as well as from the patients who avail health service from hospitals. A pilot study was also conducted to ensure the validity of both the schedules. The collection of data was done by using personal interview method in which pre-coded schedules have been used to obtain relevant data from the sample respondents. The data collected were mostly primary in nature. It is observed that many of the questions in the interview schedules were directed towards obtaining the views of both the sample provider respondents and patient respondents in different degrees of agreement or disagreement by using suitable scaling techniques.

TOOLS OF ANALYSIS

The data collected have been processed and transcribed into "Transcription sheets". To find out the patients' level of attitude towards the health services provided by the hospitals, chi-square test has been used. To find out the factors motivating the decision-making in choosing a Government / private hospital, factor analysis has been administered. To find out the discriminating variables leading to selection decision of choosing a Government or a private hospital, discriminant analysis has been used. In order to find out the relationship between selection decision factors and the overall decision behaviour of the patients, multiple regression has been applied Garrett ranking technique has been used to analyse the problems that have been faced by the patients as well as the providers of health service. Percentage analysis has also been used to find out the percentage of cost and return of hospital services and to draw inferences.

LIMITATIONS OF THE STUDY

The following are the limitations of the study:

1. The concept of marketing is new to hospital services in India and accordingly the literature available in this area is limited.
2. This study is confined to allopathic medical service only and therefore alternative medicinal treatments such as Ayurveda, Homoeopathy, Siddha and Unani have not been included.
3. The study is limited to four allopathic medical services namely Maternity, Paediatric, Orthopaedic and General Medicine only.
4. In the case of assessing the cost of health service and cost and return analysis of service providers, only the providers of private health sector have been taken into account.

CHAPTER SCHEME

The present study entitled "Marketing of Professional Services with Particular Reference to Hospitals in Kanyakumari district" has been organised in six chapters.

The first chapter titled "Introduction and Design of the study" covers introduction, statement of the problem, review of literature, scope, objectives of the study, hypotheses, operational definition of concepts, methodology, sampling design, construction of tools, geographical area, period of study, field work, tools of analysis, limitations of the study and chapter scheme.

The second chapter, "Profile of health service in Kanyakumari district and socio-economic conditions of the sample respondents" presents the overall view of the healthcare industry at the national, state and district levels. It also presents the socio-economic conditions of the sample respondents.

The third chapter, "Marketing of hospital services" includes factors involved in choosing a govt. hospital or a private hospital, factors influencing decision-making and factors discriminating public and private hospital services.

The fourth chapter, "Attitude of the patients towards marketing of hospital services" identifies the various levels of attitude of the patient respondents towards marketing of the hospital services and also examines whether there exists a significant relationship between patients' socio-economic conditions, and their level of attitude towards health services rendered by hospitals in Kanyakumari district.

The fifth chapter, "The costs and returns analysis of hospital services" assesses the costs of providing health services and includes costs and returns analysis of private health service providers.

The sixth chapter, "Summary of Findings, Suggestions and Conclusion" gives a full list of the major findings of the study and puts forth some suggestions and ends with a conclusion.

REFERENCES

1. George Joseph, John Desrochers, Mariamma Kalathil. 1978. *Health Care in India,* Centre for Social Action, Bangalore, p. 3.
2. Govind Aptc, 2004. *Services Marketing,* Oxford University Press, New Delhi, p. 4.
3. Harish V. Verma, *Services Marketing — Text and Cases,* Pearson Education, Delhi, p. 2.
4. Seema Joshi, 2006. From Conventional to New Services, *The Indian Journal of Labour Economics,* Vol. 49, p. 321.

5. In Jugaad Land, Cover Feature, Healthcare, *The Week*, August 31, 2008, p. 24.
6. *Ibid.*, p. 25.
7. Valarie A. Zeithaml, Mary Jo Bitner, 2003, *Services Marketing — Integrating Customer Focus Across the Firm*, Tata Mac Graw-Hill Publishing Company Limited, New Delhi, p. 11.
8. Angela M. Rushton and David J. Carson, 1985. The Mmarketing of Services; Managing the Intangibles, *European Journal of Marketing*, Vol. 19, No. 3, p. 18.
9. Philip Kotler and Paul N. Bloom, *Marketing Professional Services*, Prentice Hall Inc, Englewood Cliffs, New Jersey, p. 2.
10. Evert Gummesson, Senior Management Consultant, Ekonomisk Fovetagledning (EF) AB-European "How Professional Services are Bought"—*Journal of Markeing*, p. 33.
11. Bharati Rawla, New Delhi and Madhavi Irani, Bombay The Health Proposition, *The Economic Times*, Brand Equity, Wednesday-4th May, 1994, p. 1.
12. Horace E. Johns and H. Ronald Moser, 1988. How Consumers View Hospital Advertising, *Journal of Hospital Marketing* — Vol. 3, No. 1, p. 124.
13. Pat Weymes, 1990. *How to Perfect Your Selling Skills*, Wheeler Publishing, New Delhi.
14. Jha S.M, 2000. *Service Marketing*, Millennium Edition, Himalaya Publishing House, Mumbai, pp. 34-35.
15. Philip Kotler and Richard A. Connor 1977. Marketing Professional Services, *Journal of Marketing*, HD 32/9, pp. 71-76.
16. William J.Winston (U.S.A.), "The Evolution of Hospital Marketing", *Journal of Hospital Marketing*, Volume 1 (1/2) Fall/Winter 1986, pp. 19-29.
17 Rajan Modhok. Quality of Hospital Service: A Study Comparing 'Asian' and 'Non-Asian' Patients in Middlebrough, *Journal of Public Health*, Vol. 14, No. 3, pp. 271-279.
18 Baba Wazzan, 2000. Patient Loyalty Versus Satisfaction: Implications for Quality and Marketing Strategies, *Managing Service Quality*, Vol. 9, No. 4, pp. 230-240.
19 Russ, Kenneth Randall, 2006. *Consumer Expectation Formation in Health Care Service: A Psycho-social Model*, Louisiana State University and Agricultural & Mechanical College, pp. 78-149.
20 Rahman, Mohammed, A. 2006. *Measuring and Explaining the Managerial Efficiency of Private Medical Clinics in Bangladesh: An*

Exploratory Study, Brandes University, The Heller School for Social Policy and Management, pp. 84-152.

21. Rick, K. Homan and Thangappan, K.R. 1999. *An Examination of Public and Private Sector Sources of Inpatient Care in Trivandrum District, Kerala (India)*, Achuta Menon Centre for Health Services, Thiruvananthapuram, Kerala, pp. 27-85.

22 Muraleedharan, V.R. 1999. Characteristics and Structure of Private Hospital Sector in Urban India: a study of Madras City, *Small Applied Area Research Paper*, 5, pp. 47-89.

23 Bhat Ramesh, 1999. Characteristics of Private Medical Practice in India: A Provider Perspective, *Health Policy and Planning*, Vol. 14, No. 1, pp. 26-37.

24 Sbenoy, 1999. Determinants of Access to and Utilization of Health Care Services in Kerala, *Clinical Epidemiology Resource and Training Centre*, Medical College, Thiruvananthapuram, pp. 47-89.

25 Singh, D.R., Sunaina, 2005. Management of Health Care Service Sector — A Study on Primary Hhealth Centres, *Indian Journal of Marketing*, pp. 31-38.

26 Yesudian, C.A.K. 2006. Behaviour of the Private Sector in the Health Service Market of Bombay, *Department of Health Services Studies*, TISS, Bombay, pp. 33-72.

27 Mittal, M.P. and Saxena, P.P. 1974. "A Mathematical Expression for Cost and Analysis of Farm Equipments", *Indian Journal of Agricultural Economics*, 29(1), p. 51.

28 Mohan, C.K. 1973. *Production, Marketing and Price Behaviour of Pepper in Vazhoor Block of Kerala State*, Unpublished M.Sc (Agri) thesis submitted to Tamil Nadu Agricultural University, Coimbatore, p. 28.

29 "Studies on the Economics of Farm Management in Tanjore, Report for the Year 1969-70", *Directorate of Economics and Statistics*, Ministry of Agriculture and Irrigation, Government of India, New Delhi, 1974, p. 23.

30 Studies on Economics of Management in Coimbatore District, Tamil Nadu, *Directorate of Economics and Statistics*, 1971-72, New Delhi, p. 240.

CHAPTER 2

Profile of Health Services in Kanyakumari District and Socio-economic Conditions of the Sample Patient Respondents

INTRODUCTION

This part of the study includes general profile of the district, health care services—world scenario, healthcare services industry in India, India's healthcare infrastructure, rural healthcare system in India, medical tourism, healthcare infrastructure in Tamil Nadu and the profile of health services in Kanyakumari district. Further, this chapter also deals with the socio-economic profile of the sample patient respondents. Percentage analysis was used to determine whether there is any relationship between the sample patient respondents' socio-economic profile and their choice of Government/ private hospitals.

GENERAL PROFILE OF THE DISTRICT

Kanyakumari District is named after the goddess "Kanyakumari". The district lies at the southern most tip of the Indian peninsula, where the Indian Ocean, the Arabian Sea and the Bay of Bengal confluence.

Kanyakumari District is the smallest district in Tamil Nadu. Even though it is the smallest in terms of area (1672 sq.kms), its density of population is the highest in Tamil Nadu next to Chennai and in literacy it stands first.[1]

The district is surrounded by Thirunelveli district in the north and north east, Kerala state in the North West and the confluence of the Arabian Sea in the west, Indian Ocean in the south and the Gulf of Mannar in the east.

The district is bifurcated into two revenue divisions Padmanabhapuram and Nagercoil having the headquarters at Thuckalai and Nagercoil respectively. There are four taluks namely, Vilavancode taluk, Kalkulam taluk, Agasteeswaram taluk and Thovalai taluk. The district consists of four municipalities Nagercoil municipality, Padmanabhapuram municipality, Colachel municipality and Kuzhithurai municipality and also nine development blocks.

The total population of the district as per 2001 census is 16,76,034.[2]

The district is purely agricultural and its economy solely depends on agricultural production. It is industrially very backward indeed. Based on the topography, the district can be divided into three areas — namely, mountainous terrain, plain lands and undulating valley.

Next to Agriculture, the important occupation of the people of Kanyakumari district is fishing. A meager 10 per cent of the population is engaged in handloom industry. Coir manufacturing in the district is also worth being mentioned. Palmyrah production has almost dwindled in view of scarce palmyrah climbers and also the minimum palmyrah crop area in this district. As a major source of private sector employment, more than 30,000 female employees are employed in the cashewnut industry.

Kanyakumari district has many important tourist spots which can be classified as places of religious tourism, historical tourism, man-made attractions, nature tourism such as waterfalls, bird watching and wildlife sanctuaries, medical tourism and heritage tourism. Kanyakumari district has many temples, churches and mosques of historical importance attracting tourists all over India as well as from abroad.

The Government Medical College at Asaripallam is functioning since 2003-2004, with a strength of 100 students.

This district has one Medical College, 19 private Arts and Science Colleges, 10 sel-financed Engineering Colleges, 9 Polytechnic Colleges, 166 Higher Secondary Schools and 196 High Schools, contributing to nearly cent per cent literacy in this district.

HEALTHCARE SERVICES: WORLD SCENARIO

Health is the state of complete physical, mental, social and spiritual well-being, and not merely an absence of disease or infirmity.[3]

Recent statistics indicate that the overall incidence of diseases worldwide has not come down significantly. In fact, it has been on the increase despite huge expenditure on research.[4]

Poor health literacy and limited proficiency in English result in unsafe medication. Health literacy is the ability to read, understand, and act on health information in order to make appropriate health decision. Poor health literacy results in medication errors, impaired ability to remember and follow treatment recommendation, and reduced ability to navigate within the healthcare system. Hence, the rate of education has been considered as a key tool in reducing the vulnerable position of millions of people all over the world.[5] Healthcare systems around the world are struggling to meet the needs of the people depending upon them. One of the most critical challenges these systems face is a shortage of healthcare professionals.

The estimates of nurses and physicians per 1,00,000 population in selected developing and developed countries are presented in Table 2.1.

It could be seen from Table 2.1 that the estimates of nurses and physicians per 100,000 populations in India is 45 and 48 respectively as on year 1992. Further, it could be inferred from the table that India lags behind as regards to estimates of nurses and physicians per 100,000 populations in several other developing countries like Kenya and South Africa.

Table 2.1 : World Health Organization's Estimates of Nurses and Physicians per 100,000 Population in Selected Developing and Developed Countries

Country	Nurses per 100,000 population (year)	Physicians per 100,000 population (year)
Developing Countries		
1. Liberia	5.9 (1997)	2.3 (1997)
2. Ghana	6.2 (1996)	7.0 (1996)
3. Central African Republic	8.8 (1995)	3.5 (1995)
4. Pakistan	34.0 (1996)	57.0 (1997)
5. India	45.0 (1992)	48.0 (1992)
6. Nigeria	66.1 (1995)	18.5 (1995)
7. Kenya	90.1 (1995)	13.2 (1995)
8. Botswana	219.1 (1994)	23.8 (1994)
9. Bahamas	229.7 (1996)	151.8 (1996)
10. Trinidad and Tobago	286.8 (1994)	78.8 (1994)
11. South Africa	471.8 (1996)	56.3 (1996)
Developed Countries		
12. United Kingdom	497.0 (1989)	164.0 (1983)
13. Australia	830.0 (1990)	240.0 (1998)
14. Canada	897.1 (1996)	229.1 (1995)
15. United States	972.0 (1996)	279.0 (1995)

Source: WHO, 2004

EVOLUTION OF THE HEALTHCARE SERVICES INDUSTRY IN INDIA

Ancient Indian physicians attached great importance to the role of cleanliness, appropriate diet, and regularity of habits and physical exercise to keep one healthy and free from diseases.[6] India's healthcare industry is worth $23 billion today or roughly 4 per cent of the GDP. The increasing private sector participation in healthcare services is stimulating a great change in the Indian healthcare industry. According to an ICRA industry report on healthcare, India spends 5.1 per cent of its GDP on health.[7] The various services sector in India are presented in Table 2.2.

Table 2.2 : Service Sectors in India

Sl. No.	Sector	Direct Employment (2000-01)		Revenue (2000-01)	
		(In Million)	Percentage	GDP %	Percentage
1.	Healthcare	4.0	25.00	5.2	23.32
2.	Education	5.3	33.13	4.8	21.52
3.	Retail Banking	1.3	6.25	3.5	15.70
4.	Power	1.2	7.50	3.0	13.55
5.	Railways	1.6	10.00	1.8	8.07
6.	Telecom	0.8	5.00	1.4	6.38
7.	Hotels, Restaurant	1.7	10.62	0.9	4.64
8.	IT	0.4	2.50	1.7	7.62
	Total	**16.00**	**100.00**	**22.3**	**100.00**

Source: www.insead.edu

It is evident from Table 2.2 that the healthcare is the largest service industry in terms of revenues and the second largest after education in terms of employment and hence attracts the immediate attention of policy makers.

HEALTH INFRASTRUCTURE IN INDIA

One of the important indicators of the economic development of the country is the health status of the residents of the country. The developed countries have excellent medical and health related programmes. These countries have high life expectancy, low infant mortality and more per capita doctors.[8]

Healthcare in India is basically urban area oriented. Two-thirds of the hospitals are located in urban areas, accounting for nearly four-fifths of the beds. There is an uneven distribution of hospitals and beds between urban and rural areas. Just one-fifth of the beds are in the rural areas. Considering India as a developing country, the number of doctors per lakh of population is satisfactory. However, considering the rate of absorption of medical technology in this country, this ratio, 48, is quite low, compared to 251 in developed countries.[9] Some of the factors responsible for poor national health status are: illiteracy, poverty and increased population growth.

The responsibility for the present poor state of India's health services lies squarely with the political leadership, particularly with the ministers of health at the central and state levels, from the present back to the Independence period. Those ministers have consistently failed to develop the vision of the Health Survey and Development (Bhore) Committee (7) to provide integrated public health services to the people, particularly to the more than four-fifths of the population do not have the minimum necessary condition for healthful living.[10]

Health Service: An Indian Perspective

Only a few Indians go for periodic or preventive check ups. Generally they go to the doctor when they have problems. In India because of the low income, the consumer expenditure on health is very low. There is lack of awareness against deadly diseases like AIDS, Cancer.[11] Researches provide clear evidences of the economic benefits of improving health. A major result is that survival rates or life expectancy are powerful predictors of income levels or of subsequent economic growth.[12] The preventive healthcare market in India has grown 25 per cent in past five years.[13]

Public Health Services

India has a vast healthcare sector, estimated at Rs. 126.27 billion in 1998. This healthcare sector is broadly divided into the public and private sectors. Public health services consist of the following 'step-up referral' network of sub-centres, primary health centres, community health centres and district hospitals; 1,40,000 sub-centres manned by two multipurpose health workers; 23,000 primary health centers (PHCs) with a medical officer, 14 staff and 4-6 patient beds, with each PHC acting as a referral unit for six sub centres; 3,000 community health centres (CHCs) with four medical specialists, 21 staff, 30 beds and basic surgical and lab facilities, with each CHC a referral unit for four PHCs; 550 district hospitals and 1,012 at the sub-divisional level.[14]

In the urban areas the network consists of urban family welfare centres for contraceptives, urban health posts and hospitals.

Rural Healthcare System in India

The healthcare infrastructure in rural areas has been developed as a three tier system as shown in Table 2.3.

Table 2.3 : Rural Healthcare System in India

Sl. No.	Name of the system	Description
1.	Community Health Centre (CHC)	A 30 bedded Hospital/Referral Unit for 4 PHCs with specialised services.
2.	Primary Health Centre (PHC)	A Referral Unit for 6 Sub Centres 4-6 bedded manned with a Medical Officer In charge and 14 subordinate paramedical staff
3.	Health Sub Centre (HSC)	Most Peripheral contact point between Primary Heathcare System and Community manned with one MPW(F) / ANM and one MPW(M)

Source: www.mohfw.nic.in

The healthcare infrastructure in rural areas is based on the population norms as shown in Table 2.4.

Table 2.4 : Population Norms of the Public Healthcare Infrastructure

Sl. No.	Centre	Population Norms	
		Plain Area	Hilly/Tribal/ Difficult Area
1.	Sub-Centre	5,000	3,000
2.	Primary Health Centre	30,000	20,000
3.	Community Health Centre	1,20,000	80,000

Source: Ministry of Health and Family Welfare

Strengthening of Rural Health Infrastructure

With a view of improving facilities in the existing rural health infrastructure under Reproductive Child Health Programme, the Government of India assists all the States in improving/ constructing labour room and operation theatre and also providing water/electricity supply in CHCs/PHCs etc. so that essential and emergency obstetric services are improved.

The progress of rural public health system, health sub centres, primary health centres and community health centres is presented in Fig. 2.1.

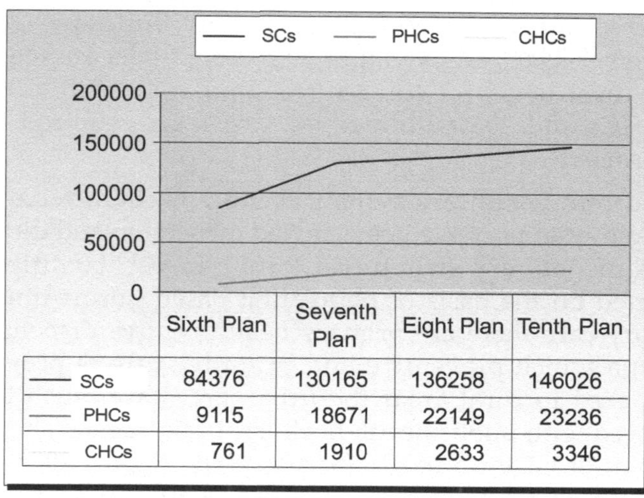

	Sixth Plan	Seventh Plan	Eight Plan	Tenth Plan
SCs	84376	130165	136258	146026
PHCs	9115	18671	22149	23236
CHCs	761	1910	2633	3346

Source: Ministry of Health

Fig. 2.1.*The Progress of Rural Public Health System: Health Sub Centres, Primary Health Centres and Community Health Centres*

Progress of health sub-centres, which is the most peripheral contact point between the Primary Healthcare System and the community, is a prerequisite for the overall progress of the entire system. As on September, 2005, 1,46,026 Sub Centres are functioning in the country. Similar progress can be seen in the number of PHCs which was 9,115 at the end of sixth plan and as on September, 2005, there were 22,236 PHCs functioning in the country.

In accordance with the progress in the number of SCs and PHCs, the number of CHCs has also increased from 761 at the end of the Sixth Plan and as on September, 2005, 3,346 CHCs are functioning. According to the figures of population based on 2001 Population Census, the shortfall in the rural health infrastructure comes out to be of 19,636 sub-centres, 4,337 PHCs and 3,206 CHCs.[15]

Building Status

About 49.7 per cent of Sub Centres, 78.0 per cent of PHCs and 91.5 per cent of CHCs are located in the Government buildings. The rest are located either in rented buildings or rent free Panchayat/Voluntary Society buildings. As on September, 2005, an overall of 60,762 buildings are required to be constructed for sub-centres. Similarly, 2,948 building for PHCs and 205 buildings for CHCs are required to be constructed.

Current healthcare system in India is characterized by multiple systems of medicine, mixed ownership and different kinds of delivery structures. Public health facilities are allocated on the basis of population based norms thus, for primary care there are primary health centres dispensaries through which preventive and primitive care is provided. Compared to rural areas the urban areas are much better endowed with public health facilities. India spends about 4.9 per cent of GDP on health (as per WHO Report 2002). It is seen that the total health expenditure is around 5 percent of GDP, Public expenditure is 0.9 per cent, Private is 4 per cent. Private health care is much larger and widespread than public

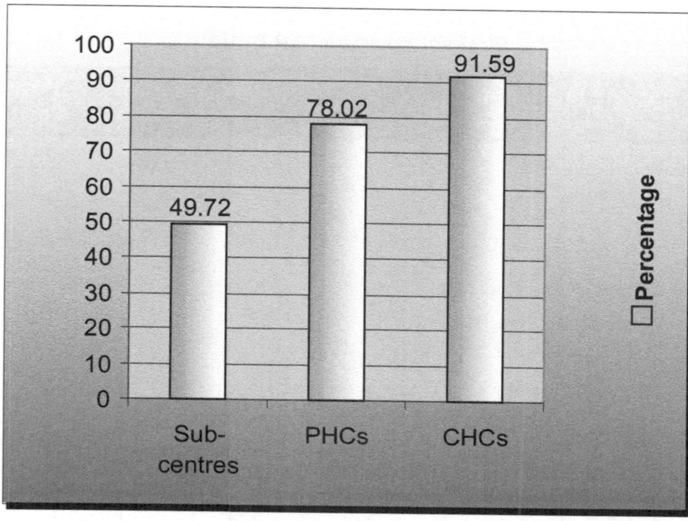

Source: Ministry of Health

Fig. 2.2. *The Number of HSCs, PHCs and CHCs functioning in Government Building in India*

health services. The number of registered practitioners is estimated to be about 13 lakhs across the country. The Allopathic doctors constitute 45 per cent of the total registered practitioners and are located mostly in urban areas, whereas non-allopathic are located in rural areas. There is no proper registration process for private hospitals. Hence, the quality of healthcare delivered by the institutions is a major area of concern. Nearly 70 per cent of all hospitals and 40 per cent of all hospital beds in the country are in the private sector. The private sector is dominant sector with 50 per cent of people seeking indoor care and 50 per cent seeking ambulatory care (out patient care) from private health facilities.[16]

The rural healthcare infrastructure in India is presented in Table 2.5. (*see table on next page*)

A Smart Approach to Public Health

The health insurance scheme for unorganised workers launched by the Government of India holds the potential to

Table 2.5 : Rural Health Infrastructure — Norms and the Present Position (All India)

Sl. No.	Indication	National Norms		Present Position
		General	Tribal/ Hill/ desert	
1.	Rural population (2001) covered by a:			
	Sub-Centre	5000	3000	5085
	Primary Health Centre	30000	20000	31954
	Community Health Centre	120000	80000	221000
2.	No. of Sub-Center per PHC	6		4
3.	No. of PHCs per CHC	6		7
4.	Rural population (2001) covered by a:	5000	3000	5574
	MPW (F)			
	MPW (M)	5000	3000	11994
5.	Ratio of HA (M) to MPW (M)	1:6		1:3
6.	Ratio of MPW (F) to MPW (F)	1:6		1:8
7.	Average Rural Area (Sq. Km) covered by a:			
	Sub-Centre			21.35
	PHC			134.20
	CHC			931.95
8.	Average Radial Distance (Kms) covered by a:			
	Sub-Centre	-		2.61
	PHC	-		6.53
	CHC	-		17.22
9.	Average Number of Villages coved by a:			
	Sub-Centre	-		4
	PHC	-		27
	CHC	-		191

Source: Ministry of Health and Family Welfare

effect a socio-economic change of far reaching significance. The Rashtriya Swasthya Bima Yojana (RSBY), launched formally last year, will provide coverage for the families of the unorganised sector workers below the poverty line. The scheme provides cashless health insurance cover up to Rs. 30,000 for all the eligible families. The smart card, which provides for the cashless transaction, can be used anywhere in the country, has the potential to open the doors of healthcare facilities to millions of the poor. It also offers a choice between public and private healthcare.[17]

Medical Tourism

The attraction of high quality healthcare facilities at comparative costs has resulted in a large number of international tourists to access healthcare services in India. Going by the current pace with which this segment has been growing, the CII-McKinsey study estimates that revenues from this segment could touch US$ 2.2 billion by 2012 (from the current figure of US$ 333 million). Indian hospitals are fast becoming the first choice for an increasing number of foreign medical tourists. India's growing reputation as a major medical tourism is attracting more and more visitors from the Middle East with many travel agents now offering packages for treatment with an added advantage of a happy vacation. In the year 2003, 1,50,000 foreigners hailing from Europe, Middle East and Canada were treated in India and thereby earned a fortune to the tune of 33 million dollars.[18] The costs of key healthcare procedures are presented in Table 2.6.

Table 2.6 : Cost of Key Healthcare Procedures

Currency: USD	US	Thailand	India	India healthcare cost-% of US
Cardiac surgery	50,000	14,250	4,000	12.5
Bone marrow transplant	62,500	62,500	30,000	13.33
Liver transplant	500,000	75,000	45,000	11.11
Orthopaedic surgery	16,000	6,900	4,500	3.56

Source: IBEF Research

Private Hospital Sector in India

The private hospital sector in India has grown without any kind of conscious state policy with regard to their size, location, personnel employed, capital invested, physical standards, service charges, nature of contracts with purchasers, information management, etc. This holds good for all kinds of medicalcare systems in the private sector. It is also true that until recently the state had not shown much interest in analyzing the nature of the private hospital sector, and in designing an appropriate policy for their growth and development. Since mid-1990s, the Government of India has been trying to persuade the various state governments to introduce appropriate and regulatory mechanisms for the private hospital sector. This includes designing physical standards for various categories of hospitals, and evolving an appropriate accreditation system, besides establishing appropriate redressal system for patients. While some initiatives have been made by various state governments and non-governmental organizations in different parts of India (including the state of Tamil Nadu) to address the above mentioned regulatory issues, as yet we do not have any state level or national level policy document that has been adopted, or being considered in consultation with various stakeholders in private health sector.[19]

HEALTHCARE INFRASTRUCTURE IN TAMIL NADU

Tamil Nadu has a well laid-out health infrastructure both in urban as well as in rural areas. The health infrastructure in the public sector in Tamil Nadu is given in Table 2.7.

In addition Tamil Nadu has a number of maternity homes, dispensaries and health posts run by the 102 municipalities and 6 municipal corporations.

The Government of Tamil Nadu is totally committed to building healthy people, not only by making available quality medicare facilities at the doorstep of every citizen even in the remotest corner of the state, but also by providing medical facilities of the highest order, keeping pace with rapid technological developments in the field of medicine to them. The Government of Tamil Nadu provides preventive, curative and promotive care to all classes of the society operating under the control of Health and Family Welfare Department.

Table 2.7 : Public Sector Healthcare Infrastructure in Tamil Nadu

Sl. No.	Particulars	No.	Range of bed strength	Total bed strength
1.	Medical Colleges	11	-	-
2.	Medical College attached hospitals	38	-	21238
3.	District headquarters hospitals	25	150 - 600	9231
4.	Sub-District hospitals	245	6 - 224	12343
5.	PHCs	1413	2 - 30	8976
6.	HSCs	8682	-	-
7.	Other hospitals (TB hospital, sanatoria, ESI hospitals, dispensaries, women & children hospitals etc.,)	NA	NA	2532

Source: www.tn.gov.in
NA - Not Available

Blood Storage Facilities Planned at Maternity PHCs

The Government will create blood storage facilities at maternity Primary Health Centres (PHC) to ensure that mothers developing postpartum haemorrhage, the leading cause of maternal mortality, get prompt access to emergency transfusion, Health Secretary V.K. Subburaj told the Hindu on the 13th November 2008.[20] Bangladesh and Indonesia have sought the help of Madurai Aravind Eye Hospital's expertise in diabetes management, and for technology to treat eye problems among diabetic patients.[21]

HEALTH SERVICES IN KANYAKUMARI DISTRICT

Kanyakumari district has contributed much to the field of Medicine. The district is endowed by Nature with several hills and mountains with rich herbs of medicinal value and also minerals. The area abounds with many unique herbs and plants believed to have originated from a small piece of the medicinal mountain *'Sanjeevani'* which fell on this place as Lord Hanuman was carrying the mountain to Sri Lanka during the war between Rama and Ravana. This part of the medicinal mountain *"Sanjeevani"* came to be known in the district as *"Maruthuvamalai"*, which literally means medicinal hill. This hill is referred to by Therapeutacs (*Buddha Bikshus)* who belonged to the period of Emperor Asoka, as having medical and spiritual heritage. Rare medicinal herbs are available here in abundance. In addition, Kanyakumari ditrict has many practitioners of various branches of ancient India's health systems like Siddha, Ayurvedha and varma kalai.

Sage Agasthiya, the first grammarian of the Tamil language was also the first and foremost of the Siddhars (the practioners of herbal medicines). He is also believed to have lived at the edge of this land there is also a village by name Agasteeswaram near Maruthuvamalai. It bears the name of the dwarf sage. In this village, there is a temple dedicated to Agasteeswaramudaiyar which is believed to have been consecrated by sage Agasthiya himself. Besides Medicine and Grammar, sage Agasthiya was also adept in Varma Sastra (the science of vulnerable points of the body). General palm leaf records like *'Varmani'* and *Varma Sastra* were written by Agasthiya. Even today, this heating art of varman treatment is taught in Kanyakumari in the Guru-Sishya tradition, and treatment is also done by elders who are quite conversant with this method of treatment. The native medicines are applied in the required proportions for treatment and several cases have proved successful. From the period of sage Agasthiya to the present day, the Siddha system of treatment has been followed meticulously by the people in Kanyakumari district.

Growth of Allopathic System of Medicine in the District

The growth of allopathic branch of medicine in Kanyakumari district is also an interesting one. The early Protestant Christian Missionaries were considered the pioneers in the field of allopathic medicine of the district. By establishing a hospital at Nagercoil, the London Mission Society (LMS) known as the Church of South India (CSI) had laid the foundation for the modern allopathic system of practice in the district as early as 1838. In due course, the allopathic system of medicine was adopted as a state system of medicine. The district owes much of its present position and importance to the efforts of the missionaries in the field of Medicine.

Present Status

After independence, the district witnessed a development of a good network of Government health care services: district hospital, taluk hospitals, primary health centres and health sub centres. Simultaneously, there had also been a constant rise in the number of private healthcare providers in the district. And when providing effective and specialty treatment was not adequate in public healthcare services in the district, the numbers of private healthcare providers began to make their mark in the district.

An assessment of the current situation of healthcare in the district shows that the organised healthcare services cater to the needs of the majority of the population especially to the people who were very poor and to those who belonged to the lower middle class. For a good number of people, private hospitals and practitioners provide healthcare services and the rest of the patients resorted to home medicinecare and indigenous medical practitioners. In today's world, people are more health conscious and are concerned about the adverse side effects of chemical drugs, and the people of Kanyakumari district are no exception. And as such, there is a section of the population which prefers traditional Indian system of treatment to the modern medicine.

Healthcare Providers in Kanyamumari District

The healthcare system in Kanyakumari district comprises Government and private sector healthcare institutions. The Government hospitals are owned, managed and controlled by the Government. The hospital of the non-governmental organizations are owned by voluntary agencies whereas the private charitable hospitals are owned by private parties.

Public Sector Health Providers in the District

The district has a good network of hospitals, primary health centres and health sub-centres providing modern method of treatment to the people. The Government has taken keen interest to render medical relief to the public under the Indian system of medicine and Homoeopathy as well. The overall public health sector's infrastructure in the district is depicted in Table 2.8.

Table 2.8 : Overall Public Health Sector Infrastructure in Kanyakumari District (2006-07)

Sl. No.	Classification	Modern Medicine	Indian Medicine				Homeopathy	Total
			Ayurveda	Siddha	Unani	Total		
1.	Hospitals	12	2	9	-	11	2	**25**
2.	Dispensaries	-	31	1	-	4	-	**4**
3.	PHCs	31	2	17	1	20	2	**53**
4.	HSCs	267	-	1	-	1	-	**268**
5.	Other medical institutions	-	-	-	-	-	-	-
6.	Bed strength	627	-	16	-	16	-	**643**
7.	No. of Doctors	169	5	25	-	30	2	**201**
8.	No. of Nurses	430	-	-	-	-	-	**430**

Source: Dy. Director of Health Services, Nagercoil
Jt. Director of Health Services, Nagercoil

The number of primary health centres with subcentres in the district is shown in Table 2.9.

Table 2.9 : Primary Health Centres with Sub-centres and Bed Strength in Kanyakumari District (2006-2007)

Sl. No.	Name of the Block/ Municipality	Name of the Block Level PHC	No. of Primary Health Centres	No. of Sub-centres	No. of sanctioned bed strength	No. of available beds at present
1.	Thovalai	C.R. Puthur	4	20	69	39
2.	Agasteeswaram	Agasteeswarm	3	27	46	46
3.	Rajakkamangalam	Rajakkamangalam thurai	3	26	15	15
4.	Kurunthancode	Muttom	4	34	9	6
5.	Killiyoor	Killiyoor	3	29	9	7
6.	Munchirai	Arudesam	4	35	18	18
7.	Melpuram	Edaicode	3	33	36	36
8.	Thiruvattar	Kuttakuzhi	4	31	6	6
9.	Thuckalay	Kothanalloor	3	32	9	9
	Toal		**31**	**267**	**217**	**182**

Source: Deputy Director of Health Services, Nagercoil

Among the 31 PHCs in Kanyakumari district, nine are main or upgraded PHCs. Each of the main PHCs is equipped with a number of sanctioned bed strength to it. But, many of the additional PHCs functioning under the control of the main PHCs do not have the number of the sanctioned beds and some of them were not sanctioned any beds at all. There are a total of 70 doctors in these 31 PHCs in the district.

Table 2.10 presents population norms and the comparative position in India and Kanyakumari District.

Table 2.10 indicates the ratio of population per PHC, CHC and the average rural area covered by a PHC and a CHC. The population covered by a sub-centre is 5,085 in India and 6,231 in Kanyakumari district. And, the population covered by a PHC is 31,954 in India and 53,870 in Kanyakumari district. These figures show a negative impact or inadequacy of the

Table 2.10 : Population Norms and the Comparative Position in India and Kanyakumari District of the Public Healthcare Infrastructure (2006-07)

Sl. No.	Centre	Population norms		India	Kanya-kumari*
		Plain Area	Hilly/ Tribal/ Difficult Area		
1.	Sub-centre	5000	3000	5085	6.231
2.	Primary Health centre	30000	20000	31954	53.870
3.	Community health centre	12000	80000	221000	-
4.	Average rural area (Sq. Km) covered by a : sub-centre	NA	NA	21.35	6
5.	Average Rural Area (Sq. Km) covered by a : PHC	NA	NA	34.20	54

Source: Ministry of Health and Family Welfare
*Compiled from primary data

Table 2.11 : Population, Beds and Doctors in Public Healthcare System between Kanyakumari and Tamil Nadu (2005-06)

Sl. No.	As per	Total beds		Total no. of doctors	
		Kaya-kumari	Tamil Nadu	Kaya-kumari	Tamil Nadu
1.	DMRS	393	21100	48	2456
2.	DPHPM	170	7191	64	2577
3.	DME	802	21833	167	4336
4.	DMRHS (ESI)	50	2363	11	642
5.	Total	1415	52487	290	10001
6.	Population (in nos)*	16,76,034	6,24,05,679	16,76,034	6,24,05,679
7.	Population per bed ratio	1185	1189	-	-
8.	Population per doctor ratio	-	-	5779	6240

Source: Compiled from DMRS, DPHRM, DME, DMRS (ESI)
*Census 2001

public healthcare institutions functioning in the study area. A comparative analysis of population, beds and doctors in public health system between Kanyakumari and Tamil Nadu is presented in Table 2.11.

Table 2.11 shows that the population per hospital bed ratio in Kanyakumari district is 1,185 as against 1,189 in Tamil Nadu. And the population per doctor in Kanyakumari district is 5,779 as against 6,240 in Tamil Nadu. Though the Government funds allocated to the healthcare sectors had always been low in relation to the population of the region, Kanyakumari district stands in a better position when compared with the other districts of Tamil Nadu as regards the population per hospital bed ratio and population per doctor ratio. A comparative description of the public sector health structure in India, Tamil Nadu and Kanyakumari is depicted in Table 2.12.

Table 2.12 : Public Sector Health Infrastructure in India, Tamil Nadu and Kanyakumari

Sl. No.	Description	India**	Tamil Nadu***	Kanya-kumari
1.	Hospitals	15,000	315	24
2.	Doctors	5,00,000	10,011	205
3.	Nurses	7,40,000	23,466	424
4.	Chemists	3,50,000	213	NA*
5.	Hospitals Beds	8,70,000	52,487	1264
6.	Primary Health Centres	23,000	1417	31
7.	Health Sub Centres	1,37,000	8,683	268
8.	Community Health Centres	3,000	NA*	NA*

Source: Assistant Director of Statistics, Nagercoil, 2005
*** DME (Director of Medical Education, Chennai-10),
** www.ibef.org,
NA* Not Available

Following the public sector health infrastructure of India, Table 2.13 exhibits the demographic scenario of India as a whole, Tamil Nadu state and Kanyakumari district.

Table 2.13 : Demographic Scenario of India, Tamil Nadu and Kanyakumari District

Sl. No.	Description	India	Tamil Nadu	Kanya-kumari
1.	Crude Birth Rate	26.1/1000 population	18.5/1000 population	13/1000 population
2.	Crude Death Rate	8.7/1000 population	7.7/1000 population	4.5/1000 population
3.	Infant Mortality Rate	68/1000 live births	30/1000 live births	7.8/1000 live births
4.	Maternal Mortality Rate	4.01/1000 Deliveries	1.2/1000 Deliveries	NA
5.	Natural Growth Rate	1.74%	1.08%	0.4%

Source: Compiled from the figures of Ministry of Health websites.

Table 2.13 indicates the demographic scenario of India, Tamil Nadu and Kanyakumari district portraying the basic health indicators. Kanyakumari district is in a better position in relation to crude birth rate, crude death rate and infant mortality rate when compared to the other districts of India and also of state's vital statistics. The adequacy of health resources in India, Tamil Nadu and Kanyakumari District is presented in Table 2.14. (*see on the next page*)

Population-to-hospital bed ratios provide an indication of the overall medical care resources, infrastructure and investments available in a local area. The population-to-physician ratio helps to assess the relative adequacy of physician services in local areas, that is, the expensive human resources waiting to attend the basic human health needs. Though Kanyakumari district is in a better position when compared with the other states in India and other districts in Tamil Nadu, it still lags behind as and when compared to the norms recommended by WHO.

Current Developments in Public Sector Hospitals

The Department of Public Health and Family Welfare in the district stands first in minimising the birth rate by

Table 2.14 : Adequacy of Health Resources in India, Tamil Nadu and Kanyakumari district

Sl. No.	Description	India	Tamil Nadu	Kanya-kumari
1.	Number of hospital beds	8,70,000	52,487	1,415
2.	Population per hospital bed	1,451	1,189	1,185
3.	Hospital beds per 10,000 population (WHO Recomm-ended 20.0)	6.9	8.4	8.5
4.	Hospitals	15,000	315	24
5.	Number of health centres:			
	(*a*) Sub-centres	1,37,006	8,683	268
	(*b*) Primary health centres	23,179	1,417	31
	(*c*) Community health centres	2,913	-	-
6.	***Human resources*** Number of physicians	50,39,000	10,011	205
7.	Population per physician	1,916	6,240	5,779
8.	Physicians per 10,000 population	5.2	1.6	1.7
9.	Nurses	7,40,000	23,466	424
10.	Chemists	3,50,000	213	NA*

Source: Compiled from the figures of Ministry of Health websites.
NA* Not available
Assist Director of Statistics Nagercoil, 2005
DME (Director of Medical Education, Chennai-10)
www.ibef.org.

recording 15.8 per cent when compared to 19 per cent in the State and 5.6 per cent in the death rate when compared to 7.6 per cent in the State and 2.4 per cent still birth rate when compared to 13.7 per cent in the State and 13.1 per cent in infant mortality rate when compared to 37 per cent in the State and 0.8 per cent mother mortality rate during pregnancy when compared to 0.9 per cent in the State and 7.8 per cent of higher order birth when compared to 16.3 per cent in the State and 65.3 per cent in the couple protection rate then compared to 50.1 per cent in the State and 88.11 per cent literacy when compared to 60 per cent in the State, said the then district Collector, B. Jothi Nirmala.

Private Sector Health Providers in the Study Area

Currently, the private sector health services range from those provided by large corporate hospitals, smaller hospitals/ nursing homes and clinics and dispensaries run by qualified personnel.

The private health care services in Kanyakumari district has grown and diversified during the last two decades. These consist of a range of players who are practitioners providing primary level care and owners of small and medium nursing homes who mainly provide secondary care and a few large corporate hospitals that provide tertiary level care. Apart from the growth of private sector in provisioning medicare, the pharmaceutical, insurance, equipment and computer software corporations have become important players in the health sector.

The hospitals and hospital beds in the private sector are skewed towards urban areas. Privatisation has influenced the perception and practice of the medical professionals. With an increased reliance on high technology, there is a greater emphasis on specialisation and a devalued role assigned to general practice. Higher salaries in the corporate sector have resulted in a movement of senior Government doctors from teaching in Government hospitals to corporate hospitals. This trend has not only been observed in big cities but in also Kanyakumari district.

The private healthcare sector includes 295 hospitals providing varied health services inclusive of nursing homes and clinics in the district. There are more than 750 healthcare professionals in Kanyakumari District. In general, the private hospitals have better infrastructure and better quality of treatment when compared to the Government hospitals.

SOCIO-ECONOMIC CONDITIONS OF THE SAMPLE PATIENT RESPONDENTS

The socio-economic profile of the members is the base for any psychological study. Especially in healthcare marketing, the socio-economic profile of the patients influences their attitude towards hospital services. It is true that there are too many socio-economic variables — nevertheless, the present study confines the variables into age, family size, gender, literacy level, occupational status, income, marital status and residential status.

Age

Age is an important determinant of the individuals' socio-economic conditions. The needs, wants and demands for health services vary in accordance with the patients' age. Consumption is largely dependent on the age at which the individual avails goods and services.[22] The age of the patients are confined into 20-30 years, 31-40 years, 41-50 years and

Table 2.15 : Age-wise Distribution of the Sample Patient Respondents

Sl. No.	Age group (in years)	Government Hospital		Private Hospital		Total
		Maternity and Paediatric	Orthopaedic and General Medicine	Maternity and Paediatric	Orthopaedic and General Medicine	
1.	20-30	34 (28.3)	21 (17.5)	38 (31.7)	27 (22.5)	120 (100)
2.	31-40	27 (21.6)	43 (34.4)	19 (15.2)	36 (28.8)	125 (100)
3.	41-50	4 (5.0)	36 (45.0)	8 (10.0)	32 (40.0)	80 (100)
4.	Above 50	15 (20)	20 (26.7)	15 (20.0)	25 (33.3)	75 (100)
	Total	**80 (20)**	**120 (30)**	**80 (20)**	**120 (30)**	**400 (100)**

Source: Primary data

•Figures in parentheses denote the percentage

above 50 years. An age-wise distribution of the sample patient respondents is presented in Table 2.15.

It could be observed from Table 2.15 that out of the 120 respondents whose age is 20-30, 55 respondents (45.8 per cent) utilized Government hospital services for curing their ailments whereas 65 respondents (54.2 per cent) utilized private hospital services. Out of the 125 respondents whose age is between 31 and 40, 70 respondents (56 per cent) utilized Government hospital services whereas 55 respondents (44 per cent) availed private hospital services. Out of the 80 respondents whose age is 41-50, 40 respondents (50 per cent) utilized Government hospital services and the remaining 40 respondents (50 per cent) utilized private hospital services. Among the 75 respondents who are in the age group of above 50, 35 respondents (46.7 per cent) utilized Government hospital services whereas 40 (53.3 per cent) availed private hospital services to get cured from their ailments.

Thus, it is inferred that whatever age group the respondents may belong to, there was no noticeable change among the respondents in availing services either from Government hospitals or from private hospitals.

Gender

Gender is a vital variable in demographic segmentation of users of hospital service. As far as healthcare is concerned, it is true that male and female have different needs and requirements. Therefore, both male and female patient respondents were interviewed in the present study. The gender-wise distribution of the patient respondents is presented in Table 2.16.

It could be seen from Table 2.16 that of the 188 male sample respondents, 108 respondents (57.5 per cent) utilized the Government hospital services to get cured from their sickness whereas 80 respondents availed the private hospital services. Out of the 212 female sample respondents, 92 respondents (43.4 per cent) availed Government hospital services whereas 120 respondents (56.6 per cent) utilized private hospital services.

Table 2.16 : Gender-wise Classification of the Sample Patient Respondents

Sl. No.	Gender	Government Hospital		Private Hospital		Total
		Maternity and Paediatric	Orthopaedic and General Medicine	Maternity and Paediatric	Orthopaedic and General Medicine	
1.	Male	24 (12.8)	84 (44.7)	8 (4.3)	72 (38.3)	188 (100)
2.	Female	56 (26.4)	36 (17.0)	72 (34.0)	48 (22.6)	212 (100)
	Total	**80 (20)**	**120 (30)**	**80 (20)**	**120 (30)**	**400 (100)**

Source: Primary data
•Figures in the parentheses denote the percentage

Thus, it is inferred from the above table that while more number of male respondents availed health service from the Government hospitals more number of female respondents availed health services from the private hospitals.

Marital Status

The marital status of the persons determines their degree of health awareness and also their level of health consciousness. It is seen that a husband shows much interest on his wife's health and vice versa. Further, parents are much concerned about the health of their children. In this study, the marital status is grouped into married and unmarried. The marital status of the patient respondents is presented in Table 2.17.

It could be seen from Table 2.17 that out of the 344 respondents who are married, 179 respondents (52 per cent) utilized Government hospital services whereas 165 respondents (48 per cent) utilized private hospital services to get cured from their ailments. Out of the 56 respondents who are unmarried, 21 respondents (37.5 per cent) availed Government hospital services whereas 35 respondents (62.5 per cent) availed private hospital services.

Table 2.17 : Marital Status of the Sample Patient Respondents

Sl. No.	Marital status	Government Hospital		Private Hospital		Total
		Maternity and Paediatric	Orthopaedic and General Medicine	Maternity and Paediatric	Orthopaedic and General Medicine	
1.	Married	70 (20.3)	109 (31.7)	69 (20.1)	96 (27.9)	344 (100)
2.	Unmarried	10 (17.9)	11 (19.6)	11 (19.6)	24 (42.9)	56 (100)
	Total	**80 (20)**	**120 (30)**	**80 (20)**	**120 (30)**	**400 (100)**

Source: Primary data
•Figures in parentheses denote the percentage

Thus, it is inferred that when the marital status of the respondent's shifts from unmarried to married they utilized the Government hospital services more frequently.

Literacy Level

The level of literacy of individuals plays and important role in their availing health services. Education plays an important role in building health awareness. The level of education of the persons gives a lot of knowledge about the medical facilities that are available at their local and distant places. In this study, the level of literacy of respondents is grouped into illiterate, up to +2, graduate and post graduate. The literacy level of the sample patient respondents is shown in Table 2.18.

Table 2.18 clearly depicts the level of literacy of sample respondents. Of the 72 respondents who are illiterate, 44 respondents (61.1 per cent) utilized the Government hospital services but, only 28 respondents (38.9 per cent) utilized the private hospital services for their ailments and of the 204 sample respondents whose literacy level is up to +2, 136 respondents (66.7 per cent) used the Government hospital services whereas 68 respondents (33.3 per cent) utilized the

Table 2.18 : Literacy Level among the Sample Patient Respondents

Sl. No.	Literacy level	Government Hospital		Private Hospital		Total
		Maternity and Paediatric	Orthopaedic and General Medicine	Maternity and Paediatric	Orthopaedic and General Medicine	
1.	Illiterate	12 (16.7)	32 (44.4)	12 (16.7)	16 (22.2)	72 (100)
2.	up to +2	52 (25.5)	84 (41.2)	28 (13.7)	40 (19.6)	204 (100)
3.	Graduate	12 (30.0)	-	24 (60.0)	4 (10.0)	40 (100)
4.	Post Graduate	4 (4.8)	4 (4.8)	16 (19.0)	60 (71.4)	84 (100)
	Total	**80 (20)**	**120 (30)**	**80 (20)**	**120 (30)**	**400 (100)**

Source: Primary data

•Figures in parentheses denote the percentage

private hospital services. Among the 40 respondents who are graduates, 12 respondents (30 per cent) utilized the Government hospital services whereas 28 respondents (70 per cent) availed the healthcare services from private hospitals. Among the 84 respondents who are post graduates only 8 respondents (9.6 per cent) utilized the Government hospital services but 76 respondents (90.4 per cent) availed the private hospital services to get cured from their ailments. Thus, it is inferred from the above table that where the level of literacy increased, they utilized the private hospitals more and where the level of literacy decreased, they utilized the Government hospital services more.

Occupational Status

Buyers' consumption pattern is also influenced by their occupation.[23] Patients' consumption pattern of hospital service is very much influenced by their occupational status. A daily wage earner may avail health service from the Government hospitals while a professional may avail health service from the hi-tech private hospitals. Thus, occupational status of individuals plays an important role in their socio-economic profile. In this study, the occupational status of respondents is classified as daily wage earners, agriculturists, businessmen and professionals. The occupational status of the sample patient respondents is shown in Table 2.19.

Table 2.19 : Occupational Status of the Sample Patient Respondents

Sl. No.	Occupation	Government Hospital		Private Hospital		Total
		Maternity and Paediatric	Orthopaedic and General Medicine	Maternity and Paediatric	Orthopaedic and General Medicine	
1.	Daily wage earners	13 (15.9)	50 (61.0)	7 (8.5)	12 (14.6)	82 (100)
2.	Agriculturists	51 (34.0)	28 (18.7)	55 (36.7)	16 (10.6)	150 (100)
3.	Businessmen	12 (10.0)	33 (27.5)	15 (12.5)	60 (50.0)	120 (100)
4.	Professionals	4 (8.3)	9 (18.8)	3 (6.3)	32 (66.6)	48 (100)
	Total	**80 (20)**	**120 (30)**	**80 (20)**	**120 (30)**	**400 (100)**

Source: Primary data
•Figures in parentheses denote the percentage

It could be observed from Table 2.19 that of the 82 respondents who are daily wage earners 63 respondents (76.9 per cent) utilized the Government hospital services for their ailments whereas 19 respondents (23.1 per cent) utilized the private hospital services. Out of the 150 respondents who are agriculturists 79 respondents (52.7 per cent) availed the health care services from Government hospitals and 71 respondents (47.3 per cent) utilized the private hospital services. Out of the 120 respondents who are businessmen 45 respondents (37.5 per cent) utilized the Government hospital services whereas 75 respondents (62.5 per cent) utilized the private hospital services. Out of the 48 respondents who are professionals 13 respondents (27.1 per cent) utilized the Government hospital services whereas 35 respondents (72.9 per cent) availed the services from private hospitals.

Thus, it is inferred that where the respondents' occupational status decreased they utilized the Government hospital services more and where the occupational status increased they utilized the private hospital services more often.

Income

Income is a vital variable affecting the socio-economic profile of individuals. It is true that individuals' spending pattern heavily depends upon their disposable income. Even though individuals pay due attention and more emphasis on their health aspect, their affordability has more say in choosing between the Government and the private hospitals. In this study, the respondents are grouped into different income groups such as respondents whose monthly income is up to Rs. 5,000, Rs. 5,000 - Rs. 10,000 and above Rs.10,000. The income-wise distribution of the patient respondents is presented in the Table 2.20.

Table 2.20 : Income-wise Classification of the Sample Patient Respondents

Sl. No.	Monthly income	Government Hospital		Private Hospital		Total
		Maternity and Paediatric	Orthopaedic and General Medicine	Maternity and Paediatric	Orthopaedic and General Medicine	
1.	Up to Rs. 5000	64 (30.5)	78 (37.1)	34 (16.2)	34 (16.2)	210 (100)
2.	Rs. 5000-10000	16 (14.3)	36 (32.1)	24 (21.4)	36 (32.2)	112 (100)
3.	Above Rs. 10000	-	6 (7.7)	22 (28.2)	50 (64.1)	78 (100)
	Total	**80 (20)**	**120 (30)**	**80 (20)**	**120 (30)**	**400 (100)**

Source: Primary data

•Figures in parentheses denote the percentage

It could be seen from Table 2.20 that out of the 210 respondents whose monthly income is up to Rs. 5,000, 142 respondents (67.6 per cent) utilized the Government hospital services whereas 68 respondents (32.4 per cent) availed the private hospital services. Out of 112 respondents whose monthly income is Rs. 5000 to Rs. 10000, 52 respondents (46.4 per cent) utilized the Government hospital services whereas 60 respondents (53.6 per cent) utilized the private hospital services. Out of 78 respondents who are in the monthly income category of above Rs. 10,000, 6 respondents (7.7 per cent) utilized the Government hospital services whereas 72 respondents (92.3 per cent) availed healthcare services from the private hospitals. Thus, it is inferred that when the respondents whose monthly income is more they utilized the private hospital services more and when the respondents whose monthly income is less, they utilized the Government hospital services more often.

Family Size

The family size of the patient respondents denotes the total number of family members living together under one roof. The family size of the respondents decides their standard of living. The consumption of healthcare service is shaped by the size of the family. Further, the members of the patient's family also exercise a strong influence in arriving at a decision as to availing of health service either from the Government hospitals or from the private hospital. In the present study, the family size of the respondents is classified into, up to 3 members, 4 to 5 members and above 5 members. The distribution of the sample patient respondents according to their family size is shown in Table 2.21.

It could be observed from Table 2.21 that out of the 156 sample respondents whose number of family members is up to 3, 56 respondents (35.9 per cent) utilized the Government

Table 2.21 : Family Size of the Sample Patient Respondents

Sl. No.	Family members	Government Hospital		Private Hospital		Total
		Maternity and Paediatric	Orthopaedic and General Medicine	Maternity and Paediatric	Orthopaedic and General Medicine	
1.	up to 3	32 (20.5)	24 (15.4)	44 (28.2)	56 (35.9)	156 (100)
2.	4-5	40 (19.2)	80 (38.5)	24 (11.5)	64 (30.8)	208 (100)
3.	above 5	8 (22.2)	16 (44.5)	12 (33.3)	-	36 (100)
	Total	**80 (20)**	**120 (30)**	**80 (20)**	**120 (30)**	**400 (100)**

Source: Primary data
•Figures in parentheses denote the percentage

hospital services to get cured from their ailments whereas 100 respondents (64.1 per cent) availed the private hospital services. Out of the 208 respondents who have family members of four to five, 120 respondents (57.7 per cent) availed the Government hospital services and 88 respondents (42.3 per cent) used the private hospital services for their ailments. Out of the 36 respondents whose family members exceed five, 24 respondents (66.7 per cent) used the Government hospital whereas only 12 respondents (33.3 per cent) utilized private hospital services. Thus, it is inferred from the above table that when the size of the family was large, they utilized the Government hospitals more and when the size of the family was small, they utilized the private hospital services more.

Residential Status

The area where individuals reside play an important role in deciding and determining their socio-economic profile. The area of residence is of either rural or urban and accordingly the patients of the hospital service are classified into rural patients and urban patients. It is true that urban patients are better informed of hospital services than rural patients. While urban patients have better exposure to modern and sophisticated medical facilities, rural patient normally do not have such exposure. In the present study, the residential status of the patient respondents is classified into rural and urban and the distribution of the patient respondents according to their residential status is presented in Table 2.22.

Table 2.22 : Residential Status of the Sample Patient Respondents

Sl. No.	Area of Residence	Government Hospital		Private Hospital		Total
		Maternity and Paediatric	Orthopaedic and General Medicine	Maternity and Paediatric	Orthopaedic and General Medicine	
1	Rural	52 (21.7)	96 (40)	48 (20)	44 (18.3)	240 (100)
2	Urban	28 (17.5)	24 (15)	32 (20)	76 (47.5)	160 (100)
	Total	**80** **(20)**	**120** **(30)**	**80** **(20)**	**120** **(30)**	**400** **(100)**

Source: Primary data
•Figures in parentheses denote the percentage

It could be observed from Table 2.22 that out of the 240 respondents whose residence is located in rural area, 148 respondents (61.7 per cent) utilized the Government hospital services whereas 92 respondents (38.3 per cent) availed the private hospital services. Out of the 160 respondents whose residence is situated in urban areas, 52 respondents (32.5 per cent) utilized the Government hospital services whereas 108 respondents (67.5 per cent) availed the private hospital services.

Thus, it is inferred that if the residential status of the respondents is rural, they utilized the Government hospital services more and if the respondents' residential status is urban, they utilized private hospital services more.

SUMMARY

This chapter aims at studying the profile of health services in Kanyakumari district and the socio-economic conditions of the patient respondents. Though Kanyakumari district is in a better position as regards population per hospital bed and hospital beds per 10,000 population when compared with the other states in India and other districts in Tamil Nadu, it still lags behind as and when compared to the norms recommended by WHO. In general, the private hospitals have better infrastructure and better quality of treatment when compared to the Government hospitals. It is inferred from this chapter of the study that there is relationship between some socio-economic variables of patient respondents and their choice of Government/private hospitals.

REFERENCES

1. Department of Economics and Statistics — Kanyakumari District, *District Statistical Hand Book*, 2007, pp. 1-19.
2. State Primary Census Abstract of Total Population - 2001, *Census 2001*, p. 16.
3. WHO, 1978, *National Academy of Psychology, India*, Vol. 51, No. 2-3, p. 92.
4. Dr. Rama Jeyasundar, 2008. Ancient vs. New Approach to Health, *KISAN World*, Vol. 35, No, 10, p. 49.
5. Balasubramaniam, B., 2008. English Language Adeptness and Health Literacy, *The Journal of English Language Teaching (India)*, Volume XLVI, Number May-June, p. 9.
6. Jeggi, 1979, *History of Science, Technology and Medicine in India*, Western Medicine in India: Public Health and Its Administration, Atma Ram & Sons, Delhi, vol. 14, p. 1.
7. Jezer Jebanesan, Babita. 2006-07, A SWOT Analysis of the Health Care Industry in Kanyakumari District, *Proceedings: Fourth Multi-disciplinary National Seminar*, SRF-2007, p. 150.
8. Rampal, M.K., Gupta, S.L. 2002. *Service Marketing — Concepts, Applications and Cases*, Galgotia Publishing Company, New Delhi, p. 513
9. Srinivasan, A.V. 2000. Healthcare in India—Profile and the Future, *Managing a Modern Hospital*, Response Books, New Delhi, pp. 23-28.

10. Debabar Banerji, 2006. Distortion of Some of the Basic Principle of Public Health Practice in India, *International Journal of Health Services*, 36(3), pp. 623-629.
11. *Ibid.*, p. 514.
12. Varatharajan, D. 2006. India's Human Development: Gaps and Prospects, *Health and Population—Perspectives and Issues:* 29(1): 1-20.
13. Sumit Ghoshal, 2008. Pre-empting, Illness, Executive Health Survey, *Business India,* September 7, p. 34.
14. R. Babita, 2007. *A Descriptive Study of Healthcare Industry in Kanyakumari District*, p. 19.
15. *Ibid.*, p. 27.
16. Priya Deshpande, 2006. Service Quality Perspective and Satisfaction in Healthcare Systems — A study of Select Hospitals in Hyderabad, *Indian Journal of Marketing,* p. 3.
17. *The Hindu,* India's National Newspaper, Editorial, 19th Nov. 2008, p. 12.
18. Gina B. Krishnan, Quality Care, Cover Story, The Check-up, *Business World,* 15 July, 2005, p. 28.
19. Muralidharan, V.R. 1999. Characteristics and Structure of Private Hospital Sector in Urban India: A Study of Madras City, "*Abt Associates Inc.*" Partnership for Health Reform Project, p. 10.
20. *The Hindu,* India' National Newspaper, Friday, November 14, 2008, p. 7.
21. *Ibid.*, p. 2.
22. Karunakaran, K. 2007. *Marketing Management (Text and Cases in Indian Context)* Himalaya Publishing House, New Delhi, p. 64.
23. *Ibid.*, p. 64.

CHAPTER

3 Marketing of Hospital Services

INTRODUCTION

This chapter deals with factors involved in choosing a Government hospital or a private hospital and factors influencing the decision of the patient respondents in availing health services either from a Government hospital or from a private hospital. In identifying the factors motivating the decision of choosing a Government hospital or a private hospital, factor analysis was used. Further, this part of the study also includes factors discriminating public and private hospital services for which 'discriminant analysis' was applied and accordingly inferences were drawn.

FACTORS MOTIVATING THE DECISION MAKING IN CHOOSING A GOVERNMENT HOSPITAL

A motive is a driving force that causes a person to take action to satisfy specific needs. By studying motivation, marketers can anlayse the major forces influencing consumers to buy or not to buy goods and services. While availing health services the factors that motivate the patients in choosing a Government hospital in the study area are classified into cost of health services, location of the hospital, pre-consultancy services, peripheral services, core services, quality of health services and familiarity with the doctors and the other staff of the hospital. Among these various motivating factors, the dominant factors were analysed with the help of factor analysis.

Factor Analysis

Mathematically, factor analysis is somewhat similar to multiple regression analysis. Each variable is expressed as a linear combination of underlying factors. A factor is an underlying dimension that accounts for several observed variables. Factor-loadings are those values which explain how closely the variables are related to each one of the factor variables discovered. Communality shows how much of each variable is accounted for by the underlying factor taken together. Rotation, in the context of factor analysis, is something like staining a microscope slide. Just as different stains on it reveal different structures in the tissue, different rotations reveal different structures in the data.[1] The amount of variance a variable shares with all other variables included in the analysis is referred to as communality. The co-variation among the variables is described in terms of a small number of common factors and a unique factor for each variable. These factors are not over observed. If the variables are standardized, the factor model may be represented as:

$$X_i = A_{ij}F_1 + A_{i2}F_2 + A_{i3}F_3 + \ldots\ldots + A_{im}F_m + V_iU_i$$

where,

X_i = ith standardized variable

A_{ij} = standardized multiple regression coefficient of variable i on common factor j.

F = common factor

V_i = standardized regression coefficient of variable 1 on unique factor i.

U_i = The unique factor for variable i.

m = Number of common factors

The unique factors are uncorrelated with each other as well as with the common factors. The common factors themselves can be expressed as linear combination of the observed variables.

$$F_i = W_{i1}X_1 + W_{i2}X_2 + W_{i3}X_3 + \ldots\ldots + W_{ik} X_k$$

where,

F_i = estimate of ith factor

W_i = Weight of factor score coefficient

k = Number of variables

It is possible to select weights or factor score coefficient so that the first factor explains the largest portion of the total variance. Then a second set of weight can be selected so that the second factor accounts for most of the residual variance, subject to being uncorrelated with the first factor. This same principle could be applied for selecting additional weights for the additional factors. Thus, the factors can be estimated so that their factor scores, unlike the value of the original variables, are not correlated. Furthermore, the first factor accounts for the highest variance in the data, the second factor the second highest, and so on.

Rotated Factor Matrix for the Variables Involved in Decision-making in Choosing the Government Hospitals

The rotated factor matrix for the variables relating to selection decision behaviour of the patients of the Government hospital is given in Table 3.1. (*see on page 64 to 66*)

Table 3.1 exhibits the rotated factor loading for the twenty three statements (variables) of Government hospitals. It is clear from the table that all the twenty three statements have been extracted into seven factors.

Factor 1

The variables defining Factor 1 with their factor loading and communality for decision making behaviour are presented in Table 3.2. (*see on page 67*)

Table 3.1 : Rotated Component Matrix for Government Hospitals

Sl. No.	Variables	Component						
		1	2	3	4	5	6	7
1.	No fee is charged for core services	.769	6.999 E-02	4.669 E-02	.230	.145	3.662 E-02	8.022 E-02
2.	The fee charged for peripheral services is very low	.686	.219	-.237	-9.957 E-02	.187	.149	.125
3.	There is no consultation fee	.617	4.832 E-02	.306	8.11 E-02	.369	3.818 E-02	2.366 E-02
4.	Medicines are available free of cost	.600	4.231 E-02	.167	.200	.348	-3.859 E-02	-.263
5.	No tips is demanded by the personnel of the hospital	.570	.277	-.222	.248	-.205	6.173 E-02	-7.334 E-03
6.	Availing health service in govt. hospital is totally cost free	.539	9.510 E-02	-2.955 E-03	.284	-.147	.325	.179
7.	All essential peripheral services are provided	-3.799 E-02	.796	6.032 E-02	.111	-.167	2.738 E-02	.109
8.	Ambulance service is provided round the clock	.259	.772	5.933 E-02	.184	-.128	-.139	.278
9.	The canteen in the hospital provides hygienic food at fair prices	6.511 E-02	.655	-.111	.136	.309	.144	2.482 E-02
10.	Laundry facility is provided	.485	.612	6.630 E-02	-6.362 E-02	.159	4.587 E-02	-6.893 E-02

Sl. No.	Variables	Component						
		1	2	3	4	5	6	7
11.	Laboratory services are rendered by trained technicians	.178	.605	.286	.277	.196	4.119 E-02	7.931 E-02
12.	The quality of core services is superior	-5.598 E-02	9.737 E-02	.849	.145	-5.637 E-02	-3.909 E-02	-4.057 E-03
13.	Core services are provided only by respective experts	-.111	-.114	.822	-6.148 E-02	.119	-.102	-1.865 E-02
14.	Core services are rendered round the clock	.258	.160	.717	1.996 E-02	-.108	.220	205
15.	All sorts of core services are provided by the hospital	7.946 E-02	.330	.523	-.156	-.196	.461	4.663 E-02
16.	The hospital is located in a highly accessible place	.127	.179	1.796 E-02	.572	.130	.142	7.815 E-02
17.	The locality of the hospital is free from pollution	.286	.244	8.172 E-02	.703	-3.984 E-03	9.389 E-02	-9.69 7E-02
18.	The doctors of the hospital are known	.188	1.321 E-02	-2.022 E-02	-3.418 E-04	.831	.215	1.303 E-02
19.	The nurses and other staff of the hospital are very familiar	.162	.135	-.146	.323	.472	-.193	.182
20.	Preliminary tests like checking of temperature, B.P. etc. can be done easily before consultation	.187	-3.847 E-02	2.721 E-02	.253	.212	.802	2.574 E-02

Sl. No.	Variables	Component						
		1	2	3	4	5	6	7
21.	Availing health care services from the hospital is safe and superior in quality	2.135 E-02	.196	.128	-7.829 E-02	7.540 E-02	2.990 E-02	.771
22.	Patient-friendly quality health service is available.	2.830 E-03	.386	-.198	.275	5.960 E-02	.369	.517
23.	Delivery of promised health service	.437	-.229	.325	.236	-4.645 E-02	-.238	.471

Extraction method: Principal component analysis. *Rotation method:* Varimax with Kaiser normalization a. rotation converged in 9 iterations.

Table 3.2. Cost of Health Services

Sl. No.	Variables	Factor loading	Commu-nality	Cronbach Alpha
1.	No fee is charged for core services	0.769	0.680	
2.	The fee charged for peripheral services is very low	0.686	0.568	
3.	There is no consultation fee	0.617	0.621	
4.	Medicines are available free of cost	0.600	0.621	0.7458
5.	No tips is demanded by the personnel of the hospital	0.570	0.558	
6.	Availing health service in Government hospitals is totally cost free	0.539	0.539	

Source: Compiled from Table 3.1

Among the variables influencing the choice of the Government hospitals, the variables such as, 'no fee is charged for core services', 'the fee charged for peripheral services is very low' 'there is no consultation fee', 'medicines are available free of cost', 'no tips is demanded by the personnel of the hospital', and Availing health services in the Government hospitals is totally cost free' constituted Factor 1 with higher factor loading. The above said six variables with higher factor loading on Factor 1 are characterised as "COST OF HEALTH SERVICES". All the six variables have high communality indicating that the variables within Factor 1 have very high association among them. The included six variables explain this factor to the extent of 74.58 per cent.

Factor 2

The variables defining Factor 2 with their factor loading and communality for decision making behaviour are presented in Table 3.3.

Table 3.3 : Peripheral Services

Sl. No.	Variables	Factor loading	Commu-nality	Cronbach Alpha
1.	All essential peripheral services are provided	0.796	0.692	
2.	Ambulance service is provided round the clock.	0.772	0.814	
3.	The canteen in the hospital provides hygienic food at fair prices	0.655	0.581	0.7078
4.	Laundry facility is provided.	0.612	0.650	
5.	Laboratory services are rendered by trained technicians	0.605	0.603	

Source: Compiled from Table 3.1

The variables such as 'all essential peripheral services are provided', 'ambulance service is provided round the clock', 'the canteen in the hospital provides hygienic food at fair prices', 'laundry facility is provided', and 'laboratory services are rendered by trained technicians' with high factor loading constituted Factor 2. The above said variables with high factor loading on Factor 2 are characterized as "PERIPHERAL SERVICES".

The higher factor loading on its variables helps in identifying variables associated with factor 2. All the variables have high communality, indicating that the variables within Factor 2 have very high association. The included five variables explain this factor to the extent of 70.78 per cent.

Factor 3

The variables defining Factor 3 with their factor loading and communality for decision-making behaviour are presented in Table 3.4.

Table 3.4 :Core Services

Sl. No.	Variables	Factor loading	Commu-nality	Cronbach Alpha
1.	The quality of core services is superior	0.849	0.759	
2.	Core services are provided only by respective experts	0.822	0.731	0.6913
3.	Core services are rendered round the clock.	0.717	0.709	
4.	All sorts of core services are provided by the hospital	0.523	0.666	

Source: Compiled from Table 3.1

It is observed from Table 3.4 that the variables affecting the decision-making of Government hospitals such as 'the quality of core service is superior', 'core services are provided only by respective experts', 'core services are rendered round the clock', and 'all sorts of core services are provided by the hospital' constituted Factor 3 with higher factor loading. The above said variables with higher factor loading on Factor 3 are characterized as "CORE SERVICES".

The higher factor loading of the variables that the Factor 3 underlies that attributes. The higher value of communality for the four variables indicates that higher amount of variance is explained by the extracted factors. The included four variables in factor 3 explain it to the extent of 69.13 per cent.

Factor 4

The variables defining factor 4 with their factor loading and communality for decision-making behaviour are presented in Table 3.5.

The variables 'The hospital is located in a highly accessible place', and 'the locality of the hospital is free from pollution' are characterised as "LOCATION OF THE HOSPITAL", and are constituted as Factor 4 with higher factor loading of 0.712 and 0.703 respectively. The communality value for the two variables is 0.588 and 0.661 respectively. Further, the cronbach alpha for these two variables is 0.6825. The high communality values of the two variables indicate that the variables within Factor 4 have very high association among them.

Table 3.5 : Location of the Hospital

Sl. No.	Variables	Factor loading	Commu-nality	Cronbach Alpha
1.	The hospital is located in a highly accessible place.	0.712	0.588	0.7132
2.	The locality of the hospital is free from pollution	0.703	0.661	

Source: Compiled from Table 3.1

Factor 5

The variables defining Factor 5 with their factor loading and communality for decision-making behaviour are presented in Table 3.6.

Table 3.6 : Familiarity

Sl. No.	Variables	Factor loading	Commu-nality	Cronbach Alpha
1.	The doctors of the hospital are known	0.831	0.773	0.7132
2.	The nurses and other staff of the hospital are very familiar	0.472	0.686	

Source: Compiled from Table 3.1

Among the variables of the Government hospitals, the variables, 'the doctors of the hospital are known', and 'the nurses and other staff of the hospital are very familiar' constituted Factor 5 with higher factor loading. The above said two variables with higher factor loading on Factor 5 are characterised as "FAMILIARITY". The higher factor loadings of the variables indicate that Factor 5 underlies the above two variables. The high communality value of the variables within Factor 5 has very high association among them. The included two variables in Factor 5 explain it to the extent of 71.32 per cent.

Factor 6

The variable defining Factor 6 with its factor loading and communality for decision-making behaviour is presented in Table 3.7.

Table 3.7 : Pre-consultancy Services

Sl. No.	Variables	Factor loading	Commu-nality	Cronbach Alpha
1.	Preliminary tests like checking of temperature, B.P. etc. can be done easily before consultation.	0.802	0.790	0.6983

Source: Compiled from Table 3.1

The variable 'preliminary tests like checking of temperature, B.P. etc. can be done easily before consultation', characterised as, "PRE-CONSULTANCY SERVICE", is constituted as Factor 6 with higher factor loading of 0.802. It is important because 'pre-consultancy service' provided by the Government hospital plays a vital role in selection decision. The communality value is 0.790. The included variable in factor 6 explains it to the extent of 69.83 per cent.

Factor 7

The variables defining Factor 7 with their factor loading and communality for decision-making behaviour are presented in Table 3.8.

It is observed from Table 3.8 that the variables such as 'availing healthcare service from the hospital is safe and superior in quality', patient-friendly health service is provided by the hospital', and 'delivery of promised health service' with high factor loading constituted Factor 7. The above said variables with high factor loading on Factor 7 are characterised as "QUALITY OF HEALTH SERVICES".

Table 3.8 : Quality of Health Services

Sl. No.	Variables	Factor loading	Commu-nality	Cronbach Alpha
1.	Availing healthcare service from the hospital is safe and superior in quality	0.771	0.663	0.7057
2.	Patient-friendly quality health service is available	0.517	0.665	
3.	Delivery of promised health service	0.471	0.464	

Source: Compiled from Table 3.1

The higher factor loading on its variables helps in identifying variables associated with Factor 7. All the variables having high communality indicate that the variables within Factor 7 have very high association. The included three variables explain this factor to the extent of 70.57 per cent.

Selection Decision Factors for Government Hospitals

Factor anlaysis of twenty three variables relating to selection decision behaviour of Government hospitals identified seven selection decision factors and the results are presented in Table 3.9.

Table 3.9 : Selection Decision Factors for Government Hospitals

Sl. No.	Factors	Figen value	Percentage of variance	Cumu-lative percen-tage of variance
1.	Cost of health services	5.612	24.401	24.401
2.	Peripheral services	2.657	11.554	35.955
3.	Core services	2.187	9.508	45.463
4.	Location of the hospital	1.283	5.576	51.039
5.	Familiarity	1.223	5.317	56.356
6.	Pre-consultancy services	1.117	4.856	61.212
7.	Quality of health service	1.082	4.705	65.917

Source: Computed Data

- Kaiser-Meyer-Olkin measure of sampling adequacy : 0.764
- Bartlett's test of sphericity : Chi-square : 3535.263
  Degree of freedom : 253
  Significance : 0.000

It is observed from Table 3.9 that the seven factors such as cost of health services, peripheral services, core services, location of the hospital, familiarity, pre-consultancy services and quality of health service were extracted out of the twenty three variables. These factors account for about 65.917 per cent of variance in the data. Eigen value for the first factor *'cost of health service'* is 5.612 which indicates that this factor contains very high information than the other factors. The first factor, *'cost of health service'* provides the maximum insights of buying decision of Government hospitals in the study area. It is a very important factor because the respondents prefer to avail health service from the Government hospitals cost free if not at a cheaper cost. The second important factor called *"peripheral services"* rendered by the Government hospital accounts for 11.554 per cent variance. The Eigen value of this factor is 2.657. It implies that patients choose to avail health service from Government hospitals because of the peripheral services available in the Government hospitals. The third factor *'core services'* accounts for 9.508 per cent variance with the Eigen value of 2.187 indicating that patients are encouraged to avail health service from the Government hospitals on the basis of core services provided by the hospitals. The fourth and fifth factors *'location of the hospital'* and *'familiarity'* account for 5.576 per cent and 5.317 per cent variance with the Eigen values of 1.283 and 1.223 respectively. It shows that patients are encouraged to avail health services from Government hospitals if the hospitals are located in a highly accessible place and when the patients are familiar either with the doctors or with the nurses/other staff of the hospitals. The sixth and seventh factors *'pre-consultancy'* and *'quality of health service'* account for 4.856 per cent and 4.705 per cent variance with the Eigen value of 1.117 and 1.082 respectively. Thus, it is clear that these factors are also important in making decision as to availing health services from the Government hospitals.

High value of Kaiser-Mayer-Olkin (KMO) test of sampling adequacy (0.764) indicates that the correlation between the pairs of variables explained by other variables and thus the factor analysis is considered to be appropriate in this model.

Relationship Between Selection Decision Factors and the Overall Decision Behaviour of the Patients of the Government Hospital

After finding out the factors involved in availing health services from a Government hospital, the next step is to find out the relationship between the selection decision factors and the overall buying decision behaviour of patients of health services in the study area. 'Multiple regression analysis' has been done to identify the relationship between the factors and the overall decision behaviour. The function in log form is as follows:

$$\text{Log } Y = \log b_0 + b_1 \log X_1 + b_2 \log X_2 + \ldots + b_7 \log X_7 + eu$$

where,

Y : Overall score on selection decision behaviour

X_1 : Cost of health service

X_2 : Peripheral services

X_3 : Core services

X_4 : Location of the hospital

X_5 : Familiarity

X_6 : Pre-consultancy service

X_7 : Quality of health service

$b_0, b_1, b_2 \ldots b_7$ are the parameters of independent variable to be estimated.

b_0 : Regression constant

eu : error term

In order to test the significance of the estimated parameters, $b_1, b_2 \ldots b_7$, t-test of the following formula has been used.

$$t = \frac{b_i}{SEb_i}$$

where,

SEb : standard error of b_i.

The regression co-efficient of the independent variables has been estimated and the results are shown in Table 3.10.

Table 3.10 : The Impact of Selection Decision Factors on the Overall Decision Behaviour

Sl. No.	Factor	Notation	Elasticity co-efficient	Standard error	't' value
1.	Overall score on election decision behaviour.	Y	—	—	—
2.	Constant	b_0	5.823	—	68.357
3.	Cost of health service	X_1	0.0825NS	0.024	1.429
4.	Peripheral services	X_2	0.1320**	0.023	5.741
5.	Core services	X_3	0.0092NS	0.0063	1.465
6.	Location of the hospital	X_4	0.1470*	0.068	2.149
7.	Familiarity	X_5	0.0725NS	0.055	1.321
8.	Pre-consultancy service	X_6	0.025*	0.010	2.395
9.	Quality of health service	X_7	0.1142	0.102	1.115

Source: Computed Data

R2 = 0.719

F-Test = 117.35

** : Significant at one per cent level of probability

* : Significant at five per cent level of probability

NS : Not Significant

It is seen from Table 3.10 that the co-efficient of determination (R^2) was 0.719 indicating that 71.9 per cent of the variation in the selection decision behaviour of the patients of the Government hospitals be explained by all the seven independent variables included in the model. The F-value indicates that the fitted log Linear Multiple Regression was significant at one per cent level and it is valid to draw inference.

Among the seven independent variables, peripheral services, location of the hospital, pre-consultancy services and quality of health services were found to be statistically significant.

It could be inferred that selection decision behaviour of users of the Government hospitals was significantly influenced by the 'quality of health service'. One per cent increase in the "quality of health service", keeping all other factors constant will increase the choosing of the Government hospital decision behaviour by 0.1142 per cent from its mean level.

The elasticity co-efficient for the variable 'peripheral services' was 0.132 which indicates that by increasing the laboratory and other peripheral services by one per cent, there will be an increase in the decision of choosing the Government hospitals by 0.132 per cent, ceteris paribus.

The variable 'location of the hospital' is one of the important factors contributing to selection decision behaviour. Its co-efficient was 0.147 and it was significant at one per cent level, indicating that one per cent increase in the proximity of the Government hospitals would increase the selection decision towards the Government hospitals by 0.147 per cent from the mean level.

The buying decision behaviour was also influenced by 'pre-consultancy services' provided by the Government hospitals. The co-efficient of pre-consultancy services was 0.025 which was significant at one per cent level. This shows that one per cent increase in pre-consultancy services of the Government hospitals would increase the selection decision by 0.025 per cent from its mean level.

The factors 'core services', 'cost of health service' and 'familiarity' were not considered as significant in the study area.

FACTORS MOTIVATING THE DECISION-MAKING IN CHOOSING THE PRIVATE HOSPITALS

While choosing the private hospitals, the factors that motivate the sample respondents are classified into quality of health services, core services, pre-consultancy services, peripheral services, familiarity, location of the hospital and the cost of health services. Among these various motivating factors, the dominant factors were analysed with the help of factor analysis.

Rotated Factor Matrix for the Variables Involved in Decision-making in Choosing Private Hospitals

The rotated factor matrix for the variables relating to selection decision behaviour of private hospitals is given in Table 3.11. (*see table on page 80*)

The Table 3.11 exhibits the rotated factor loading for the twenty two statements (variables) of private hospitals. Out of the 23 statements (variables) taken for analysis, one statement was not amenable for factor analysis and hence ignored. It is clear from the table that all the twenty two statements have been extracted into seven factors.

Factor 1

The variables defining factor 1 with their factor loading and communality for decision making behaviour are given in Table 3.12. (*see table on page 81*)

Among the variables influencing the patients in choosing private hospitals the variables such as 'availing healthcare services from the hospital is safe and superior in quality', 'patient-friendly health service is provided by the hospital', 'delivery of promised health service', 'the doctors are trustworthy, believable and honest', and 'core and peripheral services are provided by the hospital in good quality' constituted Factor 1 with higher factor loading. The above said five variables with higher factor loading on Factor 1 are characterised as *"quality of health services"*. All the five variables have high communality indicating that the variables within Factor 1 have very high association among them.

Table 3.11 : Rotated Component Matrix for Private Hospitals

Sl. No.	Variables	Component 1	2	3	4	5	6	7
1.	Availing healthcare service from the hospital is safe and superior in quality	.713	-.159	.422	-8.999 E-02	-7.423 E-02	.104	-6.546 E-02
2.	Patient-friendly health service is provided by the hospital	.661	.414	-1.405 E-02	.212	1.320 E-02	-1.121 E-02	.159
3.	Prompt delivery of promised health service	.647	.284	.203	.178	-4.492 E-02	.178	2.356 E-02
4.	The doctors are trustworthy and have believability and honesty	.629	.262	.141	.323	-2.139 E-02	-.112	.211
5.	Quality core and peripheral services are provided by the hospital	.602	7.891 E-02	-.106	.254	-4.425 E-02	-7.183 E-02	-4.760 E-02
6.	Core services are provided only by respective experts	8.256 E-02	.746	.214	-8.624 E-03	-.155	.187	-2.117 E-02
7.	All sorts of core services are provided by the hospital	.301	.715	6.856 E-02	6.432 E-02	3.043 E-02	3.340 E-03	.252
8.	Core services are rendered round the clock	3.446 E-02	.565	.470	.333	1.926 E-02	.241	-1.224 E-02

Sl. No.	Variables	Component						
		1	2	3	4	5	6	7
9.	Enquiry and reception counters are of great help	.189	.152	.777	2.928 E-02	6.516 E-02	3.495 E-02	4.995 E-02
10.	Preliminary tests like checking of temperature, B.P. etc. can be done before consultation	-1.776 E-02	.120	.531	4.327 E-02	-4.080 E-02	-1.977 E-02	.422
11.	Token system is genuinely followed without any favourtism	.405	.233	.518	9.523 E-02	6.470 E-02	.261	1.795 E-02
12.	All essential peripheral services are provided promptly	7.647 E-02	-2.078 E-02	-.340	.716	-.337	3.299 E-02	-3.976 E-02
13.	Ambulance service is provided round the clock	.247	.101	.129	.670	.123	1.460 E-02	-8.182 E-02
14.	The canteen in the hospital provides hygienic food at fair prices	.387	-4.295 E-02	.270	.542	-.224	4.227 E-02	.116
15.	Laundry facility is provided	.348	.409	.285	.523	6.793 E-02	-8.654 E.02	.254
16.	The doctors/nurses/staff of the hospital are known and familiar	-.116	-.121	-2.489 E-02	-7.047 E-02	.780	.265	1.073 E-02
17.	The doctors of the hospital are relatives	-.337	4.410 E-02	.381	-.104	.631	-.218	-1.224 E-03
18.	The doctors of the hospital are friends	.304	-.162	1.309 E-02	9.063 E-02	.552	.102	.533

Sl. No.	Variables	Component						
		1	2	3	4	5	6	7
19	The doctors and other staff of the hospital are neighbours	.239	.390	-.216	-.109	.460	.253	-.163
20.	The hospital is located in a highly accessible place	-9.476 E-02	8.228 E-02	.210	9.012 E-02	.153	.805	-5.886 E-02
21.	The locality of the hospital is free from pollution	.162	.203	-.100	-8.661 E-02	7.988 E-02	.661	.334
22.	The fee charged for hospital service is fair and reasonable	4.956 E-04	.117	9.889 E-02	-3.320 E-02	-1.876 E-02	8.576 E-02	.764

Extraction method: Principal component analysis
Rotation method: Varimax with Kaiser normalization
a. rotation converged in 15 iterations.

The included five variables explain this factor to the extent of 72.51 per cent.

Table 3.12 : Quality of Health Services

Sl. No.	Variables	Facor loading	Communa-lity	Cronbach Alpha
1.	Availing healthcare service from the hospital is safe and superior in quality	0.713	0.740	
2.	Patient-friendly health service is provided by the hospital	0.661	0.679	
3.	Prompt delivery of promised health service	0.647	0.606	0.7251
4.	The doctors are trustworthy, and have believability and honesty	0.629	0.646	
5.	Quality core and peripheral services are provided by the hospital	0.602	0.454	

Source: Compiled from Table 3.11

Factor 2

The variables defining Factor 2 with their factor loading and communality for decision-making behaviour are given in Table 3.13.

Table 3.13 : Core Services

Sl. No.	Variables	Facor loading	Communa-lity	Cronbach Alpha
1.	Core services are provided only by respective experts	0.746	0.670	
2.	All sorts of core services are provided by the hospital	0.715	0.675	0.7052
3.	Core services are rendered round the clock	0.565	0.711	

Source: Compiled from Table 3.11

Among the variables of selection decision behaviour of the patients of the private hospital, the variables such as, 'core services are provided only by respective experts', 'all sorts of core services are provided by the hospital', and 'core services are rendered round the clock' constituted Factor 2 with higher factor loading.

The higher factor loading of the variables indicates that Factor 2 characterised **"core services"** underlies that variable. The higher value of communality for the three variables indicates that the variables within Factor 2 have very high association among them. The included three variables explain this factor to the extent of 70.52 per cent.

Factor 3

The variables defining Factor 3 with their factor loadings and communalities for their selection decision behaviour are given in Table 3.14.

Table 3.14 : Pre-consultancy Services

Sl. No.	Variables	Facor loading	Communa-lity	Cronbach Alpha
1.	Enquiry and reception counters are of great help	0.777	0.671	
2.	Preliminary tests like checking of temperature, B.P. etc. can be done before consultation	0.531	0.478	0.6981
3.	Token system is genuinely followed without any favourtism	0.518	0.568	

Source: Compiled from Table 3.11

It is observed from Table 3.14 that the variables of selection decision behaviour of private hospitals such as 'enquiry and reception counter are of great help', 'preliminary tests like checking of temperature, B.P. etc. can be done before consultation', and 'token system is genuinely followed without any favourtism' constituted Factor 3 with higher factor loading. The above said three variables with high factor loading on Factor 3 are characterised as "PRE-CONSULTANCY SERVICES".

The higher factor loading of the variables indicate that Factor 3 underlies the above three variables. The high communality value of the variables indicates that the variables within Factor 3 have very high association among them. The included three variables in this Factor 3 explain it to the extent of 69.81 per cent.

Factor 4

The variables defining Factor 4 with their factor loadings and communalities for decision making as to choosing private hospitals are given in Table 3.15.

Table 3.15 : Peripheral Services

Sl. No.	Variables	Facor loading	Communa-lity	Cronbach Alpha
1.	All essential peripheral services are provided promptly	0.716	0.751	
2.	Ambulance service is provided round the clock	0.670	0.559	0.7132
3.	The canteen in the hospital provides hygienic food at fair prices	0.542	0.583	
4.	Laundry facility is provided.	0.523	0.719	

Source: Compiled from Table 3.11

Among the variables influencing selection decision of the patient of the private hospitals, the variables, 'all essential peripheral services are provided', 'ambulance service is provided round the clock', 'the canteen in the hospital provides hygienic food at fair prices' and 'laundry facility is provided', constituted Factor 4 with higher factor loading. The above said four variables with higher factor loading on

Factor 4 are characterised as "PERIPHERAL SERVICES". The higher factor loadings of the variables indicate that the Factor 4 underlies the above four variables. The high communality value of the variables indicates that the variables within Factor 4 have very high association among them. The included four variables in this factor explain this factor to the extent of 71.32 per cent.

Factor 5

The variables defining Factor 5 with their factor loading and communality for decision-making behaviour are presented in Table 3.16.

Table 3.16 : Familiarity

Sl. No.	Variables	Facor loading	Communa-lity	Cronbach Alpha
1.	The doctors/nurses/ staff of the hospital are known and familiar	0.780	0.712	
2.	The doctors of the hospital are relatives	0.631	0.718	0.7410
3.	The doctors of the hospital are friends	0.552	0.727	
4.	The doctors and other staff of the hospital are neighbours	0.460	0.570	

Source: Compiled from Table 3.11

Among the variables of selection decision behaviour of patients of the private hospitals, 'the doctors / nurses / staff of the hospital are known and familiar', 'the doctors of the hospital are relatives', 'the doctors of the hospital are friends', and 'the doctors and other staff of the hospital are neighbours' constituted Factor 5 with higher factor loading. The above said four variables with higher factor loading on Factor 5 are characterised as "FAMILIARITY". The higher factor loadings of the variables indicates that the Factor 5 underlies the above four variables. The high communality value of the variables indicates that the variables within the Factor 5 have very high association among them. The included four variables explain this factor to the extent of 74.10 per cent.

Factor 6

The variables defining Factor 6 with their factor loading and communality for decision-making behaviour are presented in Table 3.17.

Table 3.17 : Location of the Hospital

Sl. No.	Variables	Facor loading	Communa-lity	Cronbach Alpha
1.	The hospital is located in a highly accessible place	0.805	0.742	0.6821
2.	The locality of the hospital is free from pollution	0.661	0.640	

Source: Compiled from Table 3.11

It is observed from Table 3.17 that the variables of selection decision behaviour of patients of the private hospitals such as 'the hospital is located in a highly accessibly place', and 'the locality of the hospital is free from pollution' constituted Factor 6 with higher factor loading. The higher value of communality for the two variables indicates that higher amount of variance is explained by the extracted factors. The included two variables explain this factor to the extent of 68.21 per cent.

Factor 7

The variable defining Factor 7 with its factor loading and communality for decision making behaviour is given in Table 3.18.

Table 3.18 : Cost of Health Services

Sl. No.	Variable	Facor loading	Communa-lity	Cronbach Alpha
1.	The fee charged for hospital service is fair and reasonable	0.764	0.616	0.7010

Source: Compiled from Table 3.11

The variable 'the fee charged for hospital service is fair and reasonable' characterised as "COST OF HEALTH SERVICE", is constituted as Factor 7 with higher factor loading of 0.764. The communality value for this variable is 0.616. The included one variable explains this factor to the extent of 70.10 per cent.

Selection Decision Factors for Private Hospitals

Factor analysis of twenty two variables relating to selection decision behaviour of private hospital identified seven selection decision factors and the results are presented in Table 3.19.

Table 3.19 : Selection Decision Factors for Private Hospitals

Sl. No.	Factors	Eigen value	Percentage of variance	Cumulative percentage of variance
1.	Quality of health services	5.511	25.051	25.051
2.	Core services	2.512	11.418	36.469
3.	Pre-consultancy services	1.539	6.997	43.466
4.	Peripheral services	1.425	6.478	49.944
5.	Familiarity	1.148	5.219	55.163
6.	Location of the hospital	1.077	4.897	60.060
7.	Cost of health service	1.025	4.657	64.717

Source: Computed Data

- Kaiser - Meyer - Olkin measure of sampling adequacy : 0.732

- Bartlett's test of sphericity : Chi-square : 3124.294
  Degrees of freedom : 231
  Significance : 0.000

It is observed from Table 3.19 that the seven factors such as quality of health services, core services, pre-consultancy services, peripheral services, familiarity, location of the hospital and cost of health service were extracted out of twenty two variables. These factors account for 64.717 per cent of variance in the data. Eigen value for the first factor *'Quality of health services'* is 5.511 which indicates that the factor contains very high information than the other factors. The first factor *'Quality of health services'* provides the maximum insights of selection decision of private hospitals in the study area. It is a very important factor because the respondents prefer to avail health services of high quality. To improve this situation, private providers of health service shall give more importance on the attributes concerning *'quality of health service'*. The second important factor called *'core services'* accounts for 11.418 per cent variance. The Eigen value of this factor is 2.512. It explains that patients choose the private hospitals to avail health service if they are satisfied with the core services provided by the hospital. The third and fourth factors, *'pre-consultancy services'* and *'peripheral services'* account for 6.997 per cent and 6.478 per cent variance with the Eigen values of 1.539 and 1.425 respectively. It shows that patients are encouraged to avail health service from private hospitals if the hospitals provide adequate pre-consultancy services and sufficient peripheral services. The fifth factor called *'familiarity'* accounts for 5.219 per cent variance. The Eigen value of this factor is 1.148. It explains that patients used to look at the familiarity factor too in arriving at a decision as to selection of the private hospitals. The sixth and seventh factors *'location of the hospital'* and *'cost of health service'* account for 4.897 per cent and 4.657 per cent variance with the Eigen values of 1.077 and 1.025 respectively. These factors are also important in making a selection decision as to the private hospitals.

High value of Kaiser-Mayer-Olkin (KMO) test of sampling adequacy (0.732) indicates the correlation between the pairs of variables explained by other variables and thus the factor analysis is considered to be appropriate in this model.

Relationship Between Decision Factors and the Overall Decision Behaviour of the Patients of Private Hospitals

The regression coefficients of the independent variables in the overall decision behaviour of patients of private hospital are given in Table 3.20.

Table 3.20 : The Impact of Selection Decision Factors on the Overall Decision Behaviour

Sl. No.	Factor	Notation	Elasticity co-efficient	Standard error	't' value
1.	Overall score on selection decision behaviour	Y	-	-	-
2.	Constant	b_0	3.506**	0.05	70.426
3.	Quality of health service	X_1	0.141**	0.015	9.583
4.	Core services	X_2	0.134**	0.011	12.493
5.	Pre-consultancy services	X_3	0.0115^{NS}	0.009	1.298
6.	Peripheral services	X_4	0.0673*	0.030	2.237
7.	Familiarity	X_5	0.07216*	0.072	1.002
8.	Location of the hospital	X_6	0.0845^{NS}	0.061	1.386
9.	Cost of health service	X_7	- 0.0952**	0.019	5.016

Source: Computed Data

R^2 = 0.749

F-Test = 103.331

** : Significant at one per cent level of probability

* : Significant at five per cent level of probability

NS : Not Significant

It is seen from Table 3.20 that co-efficient of determination (R^2) was 0.749 indicating that 74.90 per cent of the variation in the selection decision behaviour of patients of private hospital is explained by all the seven independent variables included in the model. The F-value indicates the fitted log Linear Multiple Regression was significant at one per cent level and it is valid to draw inference.

Among the seven independent variables, quality of health service, core services, peripheral services, familiarity and cost of health services were found to be statistically significant.

It could be inferred that selection decision behaviour of the patients of the private hospitals was significantly influenced by the level of *'quality of health service'*. One per cent increase in the level of efficiency in quality, keeping all other factors constant, will increase the selection decision behaviour by 0.141 per cent from its mean level.

The elasticity co-efficient for the variable *'core services'* was 0.134 which indicates that by increasing the level of quality of core services by one per cent, there will be an increase in selection decision of private hospitals by 0.134 per cent, ceteris paribus.

The variable *'peripheral services'* is one of the important factors contributing to selection decision behaviour. Its co-efficient was 0.0673 and it was significant at five per cent level, indicating that one per cent increase in peripheral services would increase selecting the private hospitals by 0.0673 per cent from its mean level.

The selection decision behaviour was also influenced by 'cost of health services'. The co-efficient of cost was -0.0962 which was significant at one per cent level. This shows that one per cent decrease in the cost of the health service of the private hospitals would increase the selection decision by 0.0952 per cent from its mean level.

The factor "familiarity" of the hospital is one of the important factors influencing selection decision behaviour of users of the private hospitals. The elasticity co-efficient for the variable "Familiarity" was 0.07216 which indicates that an increase in the familiarity of the private hospitals by one per cent would increase the selection decision by 0.07216 per cent from its mean level.

The factors 'pre-consultancy services' and 'location of the hospital' were not considered as significant.

DISCRIMINANT VARIABLES LEADING TO SELECTION DECISION AMONG THE PATIENTS OF THE GOVERNMENT MATERNITY AND PAEDIATRIC AND ALSO THE PRIVATE MATERNITY AND PAEDIATRIC HOSPITALS

The patients of the hospitals basically differ in various dimensions especially in the perception on variables leading to their selection decision. The providers of health service should know the discriminant variables leading to selection decision among the two groups of patients in order to formulate the right strategy in future. Hence, the present study has made an attempt on identifying the discriminant variables leading to the selection decision among the two groups of patients namely patients of the Government hospitals and those of the private hospitals. The discriminant analysis of the two groups has been administered to exhibit such discriminant variables. The patients are asked to rate the given seven variables at five point scale namely strongly agree, agree, neutral, disagree and strongly disagree. The assigned scores on these scales are 5, 4, 3, 2 and 1 respectively. The mean score and mean difference of the seven variables have been computed among the two groups of the patients. The 't' test has been administered to test the significance of the mean difference. The discriminant power of the variables has been computed by Wilks Lambda. The results are shown in Table 3.21.

Regarding the perception on the variables leading to the selection decision among the two groups of patients, the significant mean difference is identified in the case of core services, locality, cost, familiarity, quality and peripheral services since the respective mean differences are significant at five per cent level.

The higher mean difference is noticed in the case of the cost of health services, the quality and the core services since

Table 3.21 : The Mean Difference ad Discriminant Power of Variables Leading to Selection Decision among the Patients of the Government Maternity and Paediatric and the Private Maternity and Paediatric Hospitals

Sl. No.	Variables	Mean score of the variables among the patients		Mean difference	T-statistic	Wilks Lambda
		Government maternity and paediatric	Private maternity and paediatric			
1.	Core services X_1	4.2583	4.4833	0.2250	3.126*	0.5917
2.	Locality X_2	4.1600	4.2900	0.130	2.182*	0.9625
3.	Cost X_3	4.1502	3.7877	0.3625	7.726*	0.3358
4.	Familiarity X_4	4.4000	4.5500	0.1500	2.214*	0.9700
5.	Pre-consultancy X_5	4.1250	4.1500	0.0250	0.281^{NS}	0.8624
6.	Quality X_6	4.7000	4.9872	0.2872	4.789*	0.4163
7.	Peripheral services X_7	4.2333	4.3583	0.125	2.156*	0.4691

Source: Computed Data
* Significant at five per cent level
NS : Not Significant

the respective mean differences are 0.3625, 0.2872 and 0.2250. The discriminant power of the variables is noticed to be higher in the cases of the cost of services, the quality of services and the peripheral services since their Wilks Lambda are 0.3358, 0.4163 and 0.4691 respectively.

In total, six variables leading to the selection decision are significant. Only those six significant variables are taken into account for the establishment of the discriminant function of the two groups. The unstandardised procedure has been followed to establish such a function. The established function is:

$$Z = 1.679 + 0.740\,X_1 + 0.525\,X_2 + 0.769\,X_3 + 0.285\,X_4 + 0.539\,X_6 + 0.415\,X_7$$

The relative contribution of each discriminant variable in the total discriminant score has been computed by the product of the un-standardised canonical discriminant coefficient and the mean difference of each discriminant variable has been included in the discriminant function. The estimated discriminant coefficient and its relative contribution in the total discriminant score is explained in Table 3.22.

Table 3.22 : Relative Contribution of Discriminant Variables in Total Discriminant Score

Sl. No.	Discriminant variables	Unstandardised canonical discriminant co-efficient	Mean difference	Product	Relative contribution in total discriminant score
1.	Core services X_1	0.740	0.2250	0.1665	23.96
2.	Locality X_2	-0.525	0.130	-0.0683	-9.83
3.	Cost X_3	0.769	0.3625	0.2788	40.13
4.	Familiarity X_4	0.285	0.1500	0.0428	6.16
5.	Quality X_6	0.539	0.2872	0.1548	22.28
6.	Peripheral services X_7	0.415	0.1250	0.0519	7.47
	Total			**0.6265**	**100**

Source: Computed Data

The discriminant variables namely cost, core services and quality of services have the higher discriminant co-efficient since their discriminant co-efficient are 0.769, 0.740 and 0.539 respectively. It reveals that the above said three variables have more influence on the discriminant function to discriminate the two groups. The higher relative contribution in total discriminant score is identified in the case of cost of services, core services and quality of services since their relative contribution in the total discriminant scores are 40.13, 23.93 and 22.28 per cent respectively. The estimated discriminant function correctly classifies the two groups of patients to the extent of 91.2 per cent. The analysis infers that the important discriminant variables leading to selection decision among the patients of the Government maternity and paediatric and private maternity and paediatric hospitals are the cost of health service, the core services and the quality of services.

DISCRIMINANT VARIABLES LEADING TO SELECTION DECISION AMONG THE PATIENTS OF GOVERNMENT ORTHOPAEDIC AND GENERAL MEDICINE AND PRIVATE ORTHOPAEDIC AND GENERAL MEDICINE HOSPITAL

It is highly imperative to identify how far the patients of Government orthopaedic and the general medicine hospitals differ from the patients of the private orthopaedic and the general medicine hospitals in order to make the right policy formulation in the future. The patients are asked to rate the given seven variables at five point scale namely strongly agree, agree, neutral, disagree and strongly disagree. The assigned scores on these scales are 5, 4, 3, 2 and 1 respectively. The mean score and the mean difference of the seven variables have been computed among the two groups of patients. The 't' test has been administered to test the significance of the mean difference. The Wilks Lambda of each variable has been computed to search the discriminant power of each variable. The results are illustrated in Table 3.23.

Table 3.23 : The Mean Difference and Discriminant Power of the Variables Leading to the Selection Decision among the Patients of the Government Orthopaedic and General Medicine and the Private Orthopaedic and General Medicine Hospitals

Sl. No.	Variables	Mean score of the variables among the patients		Mean difference	T-statistic	Wilks Lamb da
		Orthopaedic and General Medicine	Orthopaedic and General Medicine			
1.	Core services X_1	3.7333	4.3333	0.6000	6.725*	0.3162
2.	Locality X_2	4.0833	4.0250	0.0583	0.730^{NS}	0.927
3.	Cost X_3	3.8750	3.3583	0.5167	5.341*	0.3791
4.	Familiarity X_4	3.5750	4.2417	0.6667	10.018*	0.2158
5.	Pre-consultancy X_5	4.0333	4.3583	0.3250	4.193*	0.860
6.	Quality X_6	3.9916	4.3165	0.3249	3.339*	0.4825
7.	Peripheral services X_7	3.8417	4.2583	0.4167	5.072*	0.777

Source: Computed Data
* Significant at five per cent level
NS : Not Significant

Regarding the perception on the variables leading to the selection decision of patients among the two groups of patients, the significant mean difference is identified in the cases of core services, cost, familiarity, pre-consultancy, quality and peripheral services since the respective mean differences are significant at five per cent level.

The higher mean difference is noticed in the case of familiarity, core services and cost of health services since the respective mean differences are 0.6667, 0.6000 and 0.5167 respectively. The discriminant power of the variable is noticed to be higher in the cases of the familiarity, the core services and the cost of health services since their Wilks Lambda are 0.2158, 0.3162 and 0.3791 respectively.

In total, six variables leading to selection decision are significant. Only those six significant variables are taken into account for the establishment of the discriminant function of the two groups. The unstandardised procedure has been followed to establish such a function. The established function is:

$$Z = 11.87 + 0.611\ X_1 + 0.366\ X_3 + 0.685\ X_4 + 0.128\ X_5 + 0.397\ X_6 + 0.340\ X_7.$$

The relative contribution of each discriminant variable in the total discriminant score has been computed by the product of the un-standardised canonical discriminant co-efficient and the mean difference of each discriminant variable has been included in the discriminant function. The estimated discriminant co-efficient and its relative contribution in the total discriminant score is explained in Table 3.24.

The discriminated variables namely familiarity, core services, quality and cost of health services have the higher discriminant coefficient since their discriminant coefficients are 0.685, 0.611, 0.397 and 0.366 respectively. It reveals that the above said four variables have more influence on the discriminant function to discriminate the two groups of patients. The higher relative contribution in total discriminant score is identified in the cases of familiarity, core services, and cost of health services since their relative contribution in total discriminant score are 34.48, 27.68 and 14.27 per cent to the total respectively. The estimated discriminant function correctly classifies the two groups of patients to the extent of 86.2 per cent. The study infers that the important discriminant variables leading to selection decision among the patients of the Government orthopaedic and general medicine and the private orthopaedic and general medicine hospitals are familiarity, core services and cost of health services.

Table 3.24 : Relative Contribution of Discriminant Variables in Total Discriminant Score

Sl. No.	Discriminant variables	Unstandardised canonical discriminant co-efficient	Mean difference	Product	Relative contribution in total discriminant score
1.	Core services X_1	0.611	0.6000	0.3667	27.68
2.	Cost X_3	0.366	0.5167	0.189	14.27
3.	Familiarity X_4	0.685	0.6667	0.4567	34.48
4.	Pre-consultancy X_5	0.128	0.3250	0.0416	3.14
5.	Quality X_6	0.397	0.3249	0.1289	9.73
6.	Peripheral services X_7	0.340	0.4167	0.1417	10.70
	Total			**1.3246**	**100**

Source: Computed Data

SUMMARY

This chapter aims at identifying the factors involved in the patient respondents choosing a Government hospital or a private hospital and also the factors influencing the patients' decision as to availing health service from Government/ private hospitals. The factor called *'cost of health services'* provides the maximum insights of buying decision by the patient respondents of the Government hospitals and the factor called *'quality of health services'* provides the maximum insights of selection decision of private hospitals by the patient respondents in the study area. In the case of patients of Government maternity and paediatric and the private maternity and paediatric hospitals the three factors namely cost of health services, core services and quality of health services have been found as the most important discriminant variables. In the case of patients of the Government orthopaedic and general medicine hospitals, there are four such factors namely familiarity, core services, quality of health services and cost of health services.

REFERENCES

1. Kothari, C.R. 2006. *Research Methodology — Methods and Techniques,* New Age International Private Limited Publishers, p. 323.
2. Henry E Garrett and Woodworth, P.S. 1969. *Statistics in Psychology and Education,* Vilcas Fetter and Sciences Private Ltd., Bombay, p. 329.

CHAPTER 4

The Attitude of the Patient Respondents Towards Marketing of Hospital Services

INTRODUCTION

In this part of the study, the attitude of the patients towards various aspects of marketing of hospital services such as location of the hospital, pre-consultancy services, core and peripheral services, transparency, quality of hospital service, hygiene conditions, hospitality, physical evidence of health service, innovativeness and familiarity of the hospital has been studied.

THE ATTITUDE OF THE PATIENTS TOWARDS LOCATION OF THE HOSPITAL

The attitude of the patients is analysed with the help of the mean score on the six factors that strongly influenced the patients. For that purpose, the mean scores on six factors are calculated from the score of respective variables in it, among the four groups of the patients separately. In order to find out weather there is any significant difference among the four groups of patients regarding their attitude towards various aspects of marketing of hospital services, the one way analysis of variance has been administered. The resultant mean score of the factors and the respective 'F' statistics are presented in Table 4.1.

The patients of the private maternity and paediatric hospitals perceived keenly on many aspects of 'location of the hospital' than the patients of the Government maternity

Table 4.1 : Attitude of the Respondents Towards Location of the Hospitals

Sl. No.	Location	Mean score				F-Statistics
		Govt. Maternity and paediatric	Govt. Ortho. and general medicine	Private Maternity and paediatric	Private Ortho. and general medicine	
1.	The hospital is located in a highly accessible place	4.1000	3.5667	3.4500	4.2333	9.097
2.	The locality of the hospital is free from pollution	3.2500	3.4333	4.5500	4.2000	30.817*
3.	The location is easily viable	3.6000	3.0333	3.8500	4.0667	19.742
4.	The location is easily identifiable	3.0000	3.2333	4.1000	3.6000	17.394*
5.	The hospital is located in a central place	3.1500	3.2667	4.2000	4.1333	26.507*
6.	The location has all facilities such as transportation and communication	3.0500	3.5333	3.1000	3.5000	4.527

Source: Primary data
* Significant at one per cent level

and paediatric, Government orthopaedic and general medicine and the private orthopaedic and general medicine hospitals. Hence, the respective mean scores on such factors in 'location of the hospital' are greater than others. The keenly perceived factors among the patients of the private maternity and paediatric hospitals are: 'the location is free from pollution', 'the hospital is located in a central place' and 'the location of the hospital is identifiable'. Hence, the mean scores are 4.5500, 4.2000 and 4.1000 respectively. Among the patients of the Government maternity and paediatric hospitals, these factors are 'highly accessible' and 'easily viable'. Hence, the respective mean scores are 4.1000 and 3.6000 respectively. Apart from these two factors, in the case of the other four factors the mean score among the patients of the Government maternity and paediatric hospitals are the least. It reveals that the patients have negative attitude towards those factors related to 'the location of the hospital'. Factors like, 'the location is easily identifiable' and 'the location has all facilities' were perceived by the patients as low. Hence, mean scores are 3.0000 and 3.0500 respectively. The factors like 'easily viable' and 'easily identifiable' were perceived as very low by the patients of the Government maternity and paediatric hospitals and next to them the patients of the Government orthopaedic and general medicine. Hence, the mean scores are 3.0333 and 3.2333 respectively. And, next to the patients of the private maternity and paediatric hospitals, the patients of the private orthopaedic and general medicine perceived equally the factors like 'highly accessible' and 'free from pollution'. Hence, the mean scores are 4.2333 and 4.2000 respectively. The significant difference among the four groups of the patients is identified regarding the perception on 'the location of the hospital' especially on factors like 'free from pollution', 'central place' and 'easily viable'. Hence, the respective 'F' statistics are significant at 1 per cent level. The analysis infers that the patients of the Government hospitals are poor in their perception of 'location of hospitals' compared to the patients of the private hospitals.

The Attitude Towards Location of the Hospital Index (LHI) Among the Respondents

The LH index has been prepared for further analysis. The LH index is calculated by

$$\text{LHI} = \frac{\sum_{i=1}^{n} \text{SALHVi}}{\sum_{i=1}^{n} \text{MSALHVi}} \times 100$$

Where,

LHI = Location of the Hospital Index

SALHV = Score on the Attitude towards Location of the Hospital Variable

MSALHV = Maximum Score on the Attitude towards Location of the Hospital Variable

i = 1...n = Number of locational variables included

In the present study, LHI is confined to less than 25, 25-50, 50-75 and 75-100 per cent. The distribution of the patients according to the LHI is shown in Table 4.2.

Table 4.2 : The Location of the Hospital Index Among the Respondents

Sl. No.	LH Index (per cent)	Number of Respondents				
		Govt. Maternity and paediatric	Govt. Ortho. and general medicine	Private Maternity and paediatric	Govt. Ortho. and general medicine	Total
1.	Less than 25	—	12 (10)	—	—	12 (3)
2.	25-50	16 (20)	24 (20)	—	—	40 (10)
3.	50-75	44 (55)	64 (53)	12 (15)	24 (20)	144 (36)
4.	75-100	20 (25)	20 (17)	68 (85)	96 (80)	204 (51)
	Total	**80 (100)**	**120 (100)**	**80 (100)**	**120 (100)**	**400 (100)**

Source: Primary data
* Significant at one per cent level

In total, a maximum of 51 per cent of the patients have LHI of 75-100 per cent followed by 36 per cent of the patients having LHI of 50-75 per cent. The number of patients who have LHI of 25-50 per cent constitutes 10 per cent of the total and only 3 per cent of the total patients have LHI of less than 25 per cent. Among the patients of the Government hospitals, the number of patients who have LHI of 75-100 per cent constitutes 20 per cent whereas among the patients of the private hospitals, it constitutes 82 per cent of its total. No patient of private hospital has LHI of 25-50 per cent whereas there are 40 Government hospital patients in this level of LHI. It reveals that the patients of the Government hospital have poor attitude towards location of the hospitals while there is a prevalence of better attitude among the patients of both private maternity and paediatric hospitals as well as the private orthopaedic and general medicine hospitals.

THE ATTITUDE OF THE PATIENTS ATTITUDE TOWARDS PRE-CONSULTANCY SERVICE

The attitude of the patients is analysed with the help of the mean score on the six factors among the patients. For that purpose, the mean score on six factors are calculated from the score of the respective variables in it among the four groups of the patients separately. In order to find out weather there is any significant difference among the four groups of the patients regarding their attitude towards the six factors in pre-consultancy service, the one way analysis of variance has been administered. The resultant mean score of the factors and the respective 'F' statistics are presented in Table 4.3.

The patients of the private maternity and paediatric hospitals had a higher degree of perception than patients of the Government hospitals and the patients the private orthopaedic and general medicine hospitals that all aspects of pre-consultancy services are equally important. Hence, the respective mean scores on various factors in pre-consultancy services are greater than the others. The highly perceived factors among the patients of the private maternity and paediatric hospitals are 'emergency cases are dealt on need basis at any time', 'appointments can be fixed telephonically with the doctors' and 'preliminary tests like checking temperature, blood pressure are done before consultation'. Hence, the respective mean scores are 4.700, 4.500 and 4.450 respectively. Among the patients of private orthopaedic and general medicine hospitals, these factors are preliminary tests are done before consultation. The token system is genuinely followed and there is no place for favouritism and therefore no chance for misunderstanding. Hence, the respective mean scores are 4.423, 4.300 and 4.267 respectively. The patients of the Government hospitals in general and the patients of the

Government orthopaedic and general medicine in particular perceived factors like token system followed by the hospital as very low. 'The token system followed by the hospitals helps to avoid misunderstanding between the patient and the hospital' and 'the token system is genuinely followed without any favouritism'. Hence, the mean scores are 2.433 and 2.600 respectively. The significant difference among the four groups of the patients is identified regarding the perception on pre-

Table 4.3 : Attitude of the Respondents Towards Pre-consultancy Services

Sl. No.	Pre-consultancy services	Mean score				F-Statistics
		Govt. Maternity and paediatric	Govt. Ortho. and general medicine	Private Maternity and paediatric	Private Ortho. and general medicine	
1	The enquiry and reception counters very useful	3.1500	3.3330	4.2000	3.9670	14.679 *
2	The preliminary tests like checking temperature and blood pressure are done before consultation	3.5500	3.6670	4.4500	4.4230	30.409*
3	The Token system followed by the hospitals helps to avoid misunderstanding between the clients and the hospitals	2.6500	2.4330	3.9500	4.0330	40.669*
4	The Token system is genuienly followed without favouritism	3.0000	2.6000	4.4000	4.3000	55.859*
5	The emergency cases are dealt on need basis at any time	3.2000	2.9000	4.7000	3.7100	56.436*
6	The appointments can be fixed telephonically doctors	3.2000	2.6670	4.5000	4.2670	56.790*

Source: Primary data
*Significant at one per cent level

consultancy service especially on appointments, emergency cases and token system. Hence, the respective 'F' statistics are significant at 1 per cent level. The analysis infers that the patients of the Government hospitals are poor in their perception of the pre-consultancy services when compared to the perception of the patients of private hospitals.

The Attitude towards Pre-consultancy Services Index (PCSI) among the Respondents

The PCS index has been prepared for further analysis. The PCS index is calculated by

$$PCSI = \frac{\sum_{i=1}^{n} SAPCSVi}{\sum_{i=1}^{n} MSAPCSVi} \times 100$$

Where,

PCSI = Pre-consultancy Service Index

SAPCSV = Score on the Attitude towards Pre-consultancy Service Variables

MSAPCSV = Maximum Score on the Attitude towards Pre-consultancy Service Variables

i = 1. . . n = Number of Pre-consulting service variables included

In the present study, PCSI is confined to less than 25, 25-50, 50-75 and 75-100 per cent. The distribution of patients according to the PCSI is shown in Table 4.4.

In total, a maximum of 49 per cent of the patients have PCSI of 75-100 per cent, followed by 48 per cent having PCSI of 50 to 75 per cent. The number of patients who have PCSI of 25-50 constitutes 3 per cent of the total. Among the patients of the Government maternity and paediatric hospitals, the number of patients who have PCSI of 75-100 per cent constitute 40 per cent to its total, whereas among the patients of the private maternity and paediatric hospitals, it constitutes 75 per cent. So also, in the case of the patients of Government orthopaedic and general medicine hospitals, the number of patients who have PCSI of 75-100 per cent constitute 23.3 per cent to its total whereas among the patients of the private orthopaedic and general medicine hospitals, it constitutes 63.3 per cent of its respective total. At the same time, the Government patients who have PCSI of 50-75 per cent out numbered the patients of the private hospitals (64 per cent as against 32 per cent of private patients). However, the number of Government patients who have PCSI of 25-50 per cent constitutes 6 per cent of the total whereas among the private hospitals none of the patients belong to this level of PCSI. It reveals the existence of poor attitude towards pre-consultancy services among the patients of the Government hospitals and better attitude among the patients of the private hospitals.

Table 4.4 : The Pre-consultancy Service Index Among the Respondents

Sl. No.	PCS Index (per cent)	Number of Respondents				Total
		Govt. Maternity and paediatric	Govt. Ortho. and general medicine	Private Maternity and paediatric	Govt. Ortho and general medicine	
1	Less than 25	—	—	—	—	—
2	25-50	8 (10)	4 (3.3)	—	—	12 (3)
3	50-75	40 (50)	88 (73.4)	20 (25)	44 (36.7)	192 (48)
4	75-100	32 (40)	28 (23.3)	60 (75)	76 (63.3)	196 (49)
	Total	**80 (100)**	**120 (100)**	**80 (100)**	**120 (100)**	**400 (100)**

* Figures within the parentheses denote the percentage

THE ATTITUDE OF THE PATIENTS TOWARDS CORE SERVICE

The attitudes of the patients is analysed with the help of the mean score on the six factors. For that purpose, the mean scores on six factors are calculated from the scores of the respective variables in it among the four groups of the patients separately. In order to find out whether there is any significant difference among the four groups of patients regarding their attitude towards the six factors in core services, in hospitals the one way analysis of variance has been administered. The resultant mean score of the factors and the respective 'F' statistics are presented in Table 4.5.

Table 4.5 : The Attitude of the Respondents Towards Core Services

Sl. No.	Core services	Mean score				F-Statistics
		Govt. Maternity and paediatric	Govt. Ortho. and general medicine	Private Maternity and paediatric	Private Ortho. and general medicine	
1.	All sorts of core services are provided by the hospital	2.900	4.500	4.650	4.433	135.06 *
2.	Core services are provided only by respective experts	3.400	2.933	4.550	4.133	65.94 *
3.	Core services are rendered round the clock	3.450	3.200	4.350	3.866	27.06 *
4.	All sorts of core services are provided under the same roof	3.750	3.400	3.600	3.700	3.22 *
5.	The quality of core service is superior	4.200	3.800	4.400	4.033	11.23 *
6.	The cost of core service is fair and reasonable	3.750	3.466	3.900	4.233	10.63 *

Source: Primary data
*Significant at one per cent level

The groups of patients of the private maternity and paediatric hospitals had a higher degree of perception on four aspects of the core services as more than the perception of the other three groups of patients. Hence, the respective mean scores on those four factors in the core service are greater than others. The keenly perceived factors among the patients of the private maternity and paediatric hospitals are 'all sorts of core services are provided by the hospital', 'core services are provided only by experts', 'the quality of core service is superior' and 'core services are rendered round the clock'. Hence, the mean scores are 4.650, 4.550, 4.400 and 4.350 respectively. Among the patients of the private orthopaedic and general medicine hospital, these factors are 'all sorts of core services are provided by the hospital' and 'the cost of core services is fair and reasonable'. Hence, the mean scores are 4.433 and 4.233 respectively. The patients of the Government maternity and paediatric hospitals perceived the factors like 'all sorts of core services are provided by the hospital' and 'core services are provided only by respective experts' as very low. Hence, the mean scores are 2.900 and 3.400 respectively whereas the patients of the Government orthopaedic and general medicine hospital perceived the factors like 'core services are provided only by respective experts' and 'core services are rendered round the clock' as very low. Hence, the mean scores are 2.933 and 3.200 respectively. The significant difference among the four groups of patients is identified regarding the perception on the core services in 'all sorts of core services are provided by the hospital' and 'core services are provided only by respective experts'. Hence, the respective 'F' statistics are significant at 1 per cent level. The analysis infers that the patients of the Government hospital are poor in their perception of the core services compared to the patients of the private hospitals.

The Attitude towards Core Service Index (CSI) among the Respondents

The CS index has been prepared for further analysis. The CS index is calculated by

$$\text{CSI} = \frac{\sum_{i=1}^{n} \text{SACSVi}}{\sum_{i=1}^{n} \text{MSACSVi}} \times 100$$

Where,

CSI = Core Service Index

SACSV = Score on the Attitude towards Service Variables

MSACSV = Maximum Score on the Attitude towards Core Service Variables

i = 1. . . n = Number of Pre-consulting service variables included

In the present study, CSI is confined to less than 25, 25-50, 50-75 and 75-100 per cent. The distribution of the patients according to the CSI is shown in Table 4.6.

Table 4.6 : The Core Service Index Among the Respondents

Sl. No.	CS Index (per cent)	Number of Respondents				
		Govt. Maternity and paediatric	Govt. Ortho. and general medicine	Private Maternity and paediatric	Govt. Ortho and general medicine	Total
1.	Less than 25	—	—	—	—	—
2.	25-50	—	—	—	—	—
3.	50-75	52 (65)	72 (60)	16 (20)	28 (23)	168 (42)
4.	75-100	28 (35)	48 (40)	64 (80)	92 (77)	232 (58)
	Total	**80 (100)**	**120 (100)**	**80 (100)**	**120 (100)**	**400 (100)**

* Figures within the parentheses denote the percentage

In total, a maximum of 58 percentage of the patients have CSI of 75-100 per cent followed by 42 per cent having CSI of 50-75 per cent. The number of patients who have CSI of 25-50 per cent and less than 25 per cent constitute zero percentage. Among the patients of the maternity and paediatric hospitals, the number of Government patients who have CSI of 75-100 per cent constitutes 35 per cent of the total whereas among the private hospital patients, it constitutes 80 per cent to its total. Likewise, among the patients of the orthopaedic and general medicine hospital, the number of Government patients who have CSI of 75-100 constitute 40 per cent of the total whereas among the private hospital patients, it constitutes 77 per cent of its total. It reveals that the patients of the private hospitals have better attitude towards core services when compared to patients of the Government hospitals.

THE ATTITUDE OF THE PATIENTS TOWARDS PERIPHERAL SERVICES

The attitudes of the patients is analysed with the help of the mean score on the six factors. For that purpose, the mean scores on six factors are calculated from the score of the respective variables in it among the four groups of the patients separately. In order to find out whether there is any significant difference among the four groups of the patients regarding their attitudes towards the six factors in peripheral services, the one way analysis of variance has been administered. The resultant mean score of the factors and the respective 'F' statistics are presented in Table 4.7.

The patients of the private orthopaedic and general medicine hospitals perceived three aspects of the peripheral services contrary to the perception of the other three groups of patients. Hence, the respective mean scores on such three factors in peripheral services are greater than others. The highly perceived factors among the patients of the private orthopaedic and general medicine hospitals are 'laboratory services are rendered by trained experts', 'all essential peripheral services are provided' and 'laundry facility' is rendered. Hence, the respective mean scores are 4.667, 4.238 and 4.066 respectively. Among the patients of the private maternity and paediatric hospital, towards factors such as 'laboratory services' and 'ambulance service'. Hence, the respective mean scores are 5.000 and 4.100 respectively. As regards one particular factor in peripheral service — namely 'ambulance service is provided round the clock' the patients of the Government maternity and paediatric hospital perceived very keenly with the highest mean score of 4.450 and as regards the factor 'the canteen in the hospital provides hygienic food at fair prices' is also keenly perceived by the

Table 4.7 : The Attitude of the Respondents Towards Peripheral Services

Sl. No.	Peripheral services	Mean score				F-Statistics
		Govt. Maternity and paediatric	Govt. Ortho. and general medicine	Private Maternity and paediatric	Private Ortho. and general medicine	
1.	High quality laboratory services are rendered by trained technicians	4.700	4.633	5.000	4.667	8.90*
2.	Laundry facility is provided	3.800	3.866	4.000	4.066	1.68^{NS}
3.	The canteen in the hospital provides hygenic food at fair prices	4.000	4.100	3.800	3.800	3.03*
4.	Ambulance service is provided round the clock	4.450	3.800	4.100	4.000	8.02*
5.	All essential peripheral services are provided	4.150	3.800	3.650	4.233	11.77*
6.	Rest rooms are provided to attendants	3.400	2.966	3.600	3.838	23.55*

Source: Primary data
* Significant at one per cent level
NS : Not Significant

patients of the Government orthopaedic and general medicine hospitals with the maximum mean score of 4.100. The patients of the Government orthopaedic and general medicine hospitals perceived the factors like 'rest rooms to attendants' 'ambulance service' and 'all essential peripheral services are provided' as very low. Hence, the mean scores are 2.966, 3.800 and 3.800 respectively. The significant difference among the four groups of patients is identified regarding the perception on peripheral services in 'rest rooms to attendants' 'all essential peripheral services are provided' and 'laboratory services' rendered. Hence, the respective 'F' statistics are significant at 1 per cent level. The analysis infers that though by and large the patients of the private hospitals have better attitude towards maximum factors on peripheral services, in the case of certain factors like 'ambulance service' and 'canteen facility' the patients of the Government hospitals have greater positive attitude when compared to the patients of the private hospitals.

The Attitude towards Peripheral Service Index (PSI) among the Respondents

The PS index has been prepared for further analysis. The PS index is calculated by

$$PSI = \frac{\sum_{i=1}^{n} SAPSVi}{\sum_{i=1}^{n} MSAPSVi} \times 100$$

Where,

PSI = Peripheral Service Index

SAPSV = Score on the Attitude towards Peripheral Service Variables

MSAPSV = Maximum Score on the Attitude towards Peripheral Service Variables

i = 1. . . n = Number of Peripheral service variables included

In the present study, PSI is confined to less than 25, 25-50, 50-75 and 75-100 per cent. The distribution of the patients according to the PSI is shown in Table 4.8.

In total, a maximum of 71 per cent of the patients have PSI of 75-100 per cent followed by 29 per cent have PSI of 50 to 75 per cent. Among the patients of the maternity and paediatric hospitals, the number of Government patients who have PSI of 75-100 per cent constitute 90 per cent to its total whereas among the number of private patients, it constitutes 70 per cent of the total. At the same time as regards, the

Table 4.8 : The Peripheral Service Index Among the Respondents

Sl. No.	PCS Index (per cent)	Number of Respondents				Total
		Govt. Maternity and paediatric	Govt. Ortho. and general medicine	Private Maternity and paediatric	Govt. Ortho and general medicine	
1	Less than 25	—	—	—	—	—
2	25-50	—	—	—	—	—
3	50-75	8 (10)	60 (50)	24 (30)	24 (20)	116 (29)
4	75-100	72 (90)	60 (50)	56 (70)	96 (80)	284 (71)
	Total	**80 (100)**	**120 (100)**	**80 (100)**	**120 (100)**	**400 (100)**

*Figures within the parentheses denote the percentage

patients of the Government orthopaedic and general medicine hospitals, the number of patients, who have PSI of 75-100 per cent constitute 50 per cent to its total whereas among the private patients it constitutes 80 per cent of the total. Thus, the study reveals that the Government maternity and paediatric hospital patients have better attitude when compared to the attitude of patients of the private maternity and paediatric hospitals.

THE ATTITUDE OF THE PATIENTS TOWARDS TRANSPARENCY

The attitudes of the patients is analysed with the help of the mean score on the six factors among the patients. For that purpose the mean scores on six factors are calculated from the score of the respective variables in it among the four groups of the patients exclusively. In order to find out whether there is any significant difference among the four groups of the patients regarding their attitude towards six factors in transparency, the one way analysis of variance has been administered. The resultant mean score of the factors and the respective 'F' statistics are presented in Table 4.9.

Table 4.9 : The Attitude of the Respondents Towards Transparency

Sl. No.	Transparency	Mean score				F-Statistics
		Govt. Maternity and paediatric	Govt. Ortho. and general medicine	Private Maternity and paediatric	Private Ortho. and general medicine	
1.	All the information regarding the services provided are adequately given to the clients	4.250	4.300	4.450	4.300	0.902NS
2.	The reasons for rendering such medical services are duly informed to the clients or their attendants	3.950	4.133	4.450	4.066	8.56*
3.	Full information about the clients' health condition is duly revealed to them or to their attendants	4.050	4.333	4.350	3.966	6.64*
4.	There is transparency in charging fees	4.050	4.400	3.600	3.667	15.05*
5.	Information about the avilability of medical experts is duly informed to the clients	3.450	3.600	4.500	4.133	20.43*
6.	Full particulars about the facilities available in the hospital are disclosed honestly by the service provider	4.200	4.166	4.550	4.133	4.93*

Source: Primary Data
NS — Not Significant
*Significant at one per cent level

The patients of the private maternity and paediatric hospitals perceived keenly on five aspects of transparency than the patients of the other groups. Hence, the respective mean scores on those factors in transparency are greater than the others. The keenly perceived factors among the patients of the private maternity and paediatric hospital are 'disclosing full particulars honestly', 'patients are duly informed about the availability of medical experts', 'informing the reasons for rendering such medical services' and 'providing adequate information'. Hence, mean scores are 4.550, 4.500, 4.450 and 4.450 respectively. Among the patients of the Government maternity and paediatric hospital, these factors are 'providing adequate information' 'disclosing full particulars honestly' and 'transparency in charging fees'. Hence, the mean scores are 4.250, 4.200 and 4.050 respectively. The patients of the Government maternity and the paediatric hospitals perceived the factors like 'patients are duly informed about the availability of the medical experts' and 'informing patients about the reasons for rendering such medical services as very low. Hence, the mean scores are 3.450 and 3.950 respectively. The significant difference among the four groups of patients is identified regarding the perception on the transparency in 'informing the patients duly about the availability of medical experts' and 'transparency in charging fees'. Hence, the respective 'F' statistics are significant at 1 per cent level as regards all the six factors excepting one factor viz. 'providing adequate information'. The analysis infers that the patients of the private hospitals have better positive attitude towards the six factors on transparency.

The Attitude towards Transparency Index (TI) among the Respondents

The TI index has been prepared for further analysis. The TI index is calculated by

$$TI = \frac{\sum_{i=1}^{n} SATVi}{\sum_{i=1}^{n} MSATVi} \times 100$$

Where,

TI = Transparency Index

SATV = Score on the Attitude towards Transparency Variables

MSATV = Maximum Score on the Attitude towards Transparency Variables

i = 1. . . n = Number of Transparency variables included

In the present study, TI is confined to less than 25, 25-50, 50-75 and 75-100 per cent. The distribution of the patients according to the TI is shown in Table 4.10.

Table 4.10 : The Transparency Index Among the Respondents

Sl. No.	TI (per cent)	Number of Respondents				
		Govt. Maternity and paediatric	Govt. Ortho. and general medicine	Private Maternity and paediatric	Govt. Ortho and general medicine	Total
1.	Less than 25	—	—	—	—	—
2.	25-50	4 (5)	4 (3)	—	—	8 (2)
3.	50-75	24 (30)	24 (20)	20 (25)	48 (40)	116 (29)
4.	75-100	52 (65)	92 (77)	60 (75)	72 (60)	276 (69)
	Total	**80 (100)**	**120 (100)**	**80 (100)**	**120 (100)**	**400 (100)**

* Figures within the parentheses denote the percentage

In total, a maximum of 69 per cent of the patients have TI of 75-100 per cent followed by 29 per cent who have TI of 50-75 per cent. The number of patients who have TI of 25-50 constitutes 2 per cent of the total and no patient has TI lesser than 25 per cent. Among the 116 patient who have TI of 50-75 per cent, 25 per cent patients are belonging to the Government hospitals and 32.5 per cent of the patients belong to the private hospitals. Among the patients of maternity and paediatric hospitals, 65 per cent of the Government hospital patients have TI of 75-100 per cent whereas 75 per cent of the private hospital patients have 75-100 per cent TI. At the same time, in the case of patients of the orthopaedic and general medicine, while 77 per cent of the Government hospital patients have TI of 75-100 per cent only 60 per cent of the patients of the private hospital have IT of 75-100 per cent. It reveals that more or less patients of both the healthcare sectors namely the public and the private have the same level of attitude towards transparency of the hospitals.

THE ATTITUDE OF THE PATIENTS TOWARDS QUALITY OF SERVICE

The attitudes of the patients is analysed with the help of the mean score on the six factors among the patients. For that purpose, the mean scores on six factors are calculated from the score of the respective variables in it among the four groups of the patients exclusively. In order to find out whether there is any significant difference among the four groups of the patients regarding their attitude towards the six factors in 'quality of service', the one way analysis of variance has been administered. The resultant mean score of the factors and the respective 'F' statistics are presented in Table 4.11.

The patients of the private maternity and paediatric hospitals perceived as highly important on all aspects of 'quality of service' more than the patients of all other three groups of patients since the mean scores on all factors on quality of service are greater than others. The highly perceived factors among 'the patients of private maternity and paediatric hospitals are the entire staff team of the hospital has willingness to help and provide prompt service', 'the doctors are trustworthy and possess believability and honesty' and 'availing healthcare service from the hospital is safe and free from risk' since the respective mean scores are 4.550, 4.500 and 4.400 respectively. The patients' of Government orthopaedic and general medicine hospitals perceived as very low the factors like 'delivery of promised services' and 'the doctors are trustworthy and possess believability and honesty' since the mean scores are 3.300 and 3.366 respectively. The significant difference among the four groups is identified regarding the perception of the quality of service in the factors 'the doctors are trustworthy and possess believability and honesty' and 'availing healthcare service from the hospital is safe and free from risk' since the respective 'F' statistics are significant at 1 per cent level. The analysis infers that the patients of the Government hospital in general and the patients

Table 4.11 : The Attitude of the Respondents Towards the Quality of Hospital Services

Sl. No.	Location	Mean score				F-Statistics
		Govt. Maternity and paediatric	Govt. Ortho. and general medicine	Private Maternity and paediatric	Private Ortho. and general medicine	
1.	Availing health care service from the hospital is safe and risk free	3.550	3.800	4.400	4.366	22.12*
2.	The doctors are trustworthy and possess credibility and honesty	3.450	3.366	4.500	4.066	39.48*
3.	The doctors take efforts to know the clients and their needs	3.600	3.433	4.300	3.833	13.27*
4.	The entire staff team of the hospital ready to help and provide prompt service	4.050	3.667	4.550	3.933	17.92*
5.	The personnel of the hospital listen to the patients and keep the clients fully informed	4.050	3.867	4.200	3.567	9.32*
6.	Deliver promised service	3.700	3.300	4.050	3.600	12.55*

Source: Primary Data
* Significant at one per cent level

of the Government orthopaedic and general medicine hospitals in specific have perceived the quality of service as low when compared to the patients of the private hospitals.

The Attitude towards Quality of Hospital Services Index (QHSI) among the Respondents

The QHS index has been prepared for further analysis. The QHS index is calculated by

$$QHSI = \frac{\sum_{i=1}^{n} SAQHSVi}{\sum_{i=1}^{n} MSAQHSVi} \times 100$$

Where,

QHSI = Quality Hospital Service Index

SAQHSV = Score on the Attitude towards Quality of Hospital Servic Variables

MSAQHSV = Maximum Score on the Attitude towards Quality of Hospital Service Variables

i = 1. . . n = Number of Quality service variables included

In the present study, QHSI is confined to less than 25, 25-50, 50-75 and 75-100 per cent. The distribution of patients according to the QHSI is shown in Table 4.12.

In total, 51 per cent of the patients have QHSI of 75-100 per cent followed by 49 per cent of who have QHSI of 50-75 per cent. No patient has QHSI of either less than 25 per cent or 25-50 per cent. Among the patients who have QHSI of 75-100 per cent the number of patients of the Government maternity and paediatric constitute 45 per cent whereas the number of patients of the private maternity and paediatric constitutes 85 to its total. Likewise while the number of patients of the Government orthopaedic and general medicine constitutes 30 per cent to its total, the number of patients of the private orthopaedic and general medicine hospital constitute 53 per cent to its total. It reveals the existence of poor attitude among the patients of the Government hospitals as regards the quality of service

Table 4.12 : The Quality of Hospital Service Index Among the Respondents

Sl. No.	QHS Index (per cent)	Number of Respondents				
		Govt. Maternity and paediatric	Govt. Ortho. and general medicine	Private Maternity and paediatric	Govt. Ortho and general medicine	Total
1.	Less than 25	—	—	—	—	—
2.	25-50	—	—	—	—	—
3.	50-75	44 (55)	84 (70)	12 (15)	56 (47)	196 (49)
4.	75-100	36 (45)	36 (30)	68 (85)	64 (53)	204 (51)
	Total	**80 (100)**	**120 (100)**	**80 (100)**	**120 (100)**	**400 (100)**

* Figures within the parentheses denote the percentage

THE ATTITUDE OF THE PATIENTS TOWARDS HYGIENIC CONDITIONS

The attitudes of the patients is analysed with the help of the mean score on the six factors among the patients. For that purpose, the mean scores on the six factors are calculated from the score of the respective variables in it among the four groups of patients exclusively. In order to find out whether there is any significant difference among the four groups of patients regarding their attitude towards six factors in hygienic conditions, the one way analysis of variance has been administered. The resultant mean score of the factors and the respective 'F' statistics are presented in Table 4.13.

The patients of the private maternity and paediatric hospitals perceived as highly positive on five aspects of hygienic conditions more than the other three groups of the patients. Hence, the respective mean scores on these factors in hygienic conditions are greater than others. The highly

Table 4.13 : The Attitude of the Respondents Towards Hygienic Conditions

Sl. No.	Hygienic conditions	Mean score				F-Statistics
		Govt. Maternity and paediatric	Govt. Ortho. and general medicine	Private Maternity and paediatric	Private Ortho. and general medicine	
1.	The surroundings and the floors of the hospital are neatly maintained	4.000	4.100	4.600	4.467	15.80*
2.	The bed spread and the pillow cover are changed daily	3.200	3.667	4.400	3.967	28.24*
3.	The Equipments used by the doctors and nurses are sterlised regularly	4.000	3.600	4.200	4.100	9.42*
4.	Proper drainage system is maintained to avoid mosquito breeding	4.000	3.800	4.300	3.800	6.04*
5.	The doctors and the nurses providing healthcare service are hygiene consi-cious and follow a befitting dress code	4.000	3.967	4.350	3.900	4.32*
6.	There is a proper disposal system for the biomedical waste	3.850	3.567	3.700	3.500	2.80*

Source: Primary Data
*Significant at one per cent level

perceived factors among the patients of the private maternity and paediatric are 'the surroundings and the floors of the hospital are neatly maintained', 'the bed spread and the pillow cover are changed daily' 'the individuals providing health care service like doctors and nurses are hygienic conscious and follow a befitting dress code' and 'proper drainage system is maintained to avoid mosquito breeding'. Hence, the respective mean scores are 4.600, 4.400, 4.350 and 4.300

respectively. Among the patients of the private orthopaedic and general medicine hospitals, these factors are 'the surrounding and the floors of the hospital are neatly maintained' and 'the equipment used by the doctors and nurses are sterilised regularly' since the respective mean scores are 4.467 and 4.100. The patients of the Government maternity and paediatric hospitals perceived the factors like 'the bed spread and the pillow cover are changed daily' and 'there is a proper disposal system of the biomedical waste' as very low. Hence, the mean scores are 3.200 and 3.850 respectively. The significant difference among the four groups of the patients is identified regarding the perception on the hygienic condition in 'the bed spread and the pillow cover are changed daily' and 'the surroundings and the floors of the hospital are neatly maintained' since the respective 'F' statistics are significant at 1 per cent level. The analysis infers that the patients of the Government hospital have poor perception over hygienic conditions when compared to patients of the private hospitals.

The Attitude towards Hygienic Conditions Index (HCI) among the Respondents

The HC index has been prepared for further analysis. The HC index is calculated by

$$\text{HCI} = \frac{\sum_{i=1}^{n} \text{SAHCVi}}{\sum_{i=1}^{n} \text{MSAHCVi}} \times 100$$

Where,

HCI = Hygienic Conditions Index

SAHCV = Score on the Attitude towards Hygienic condition Variables

MSAHCV = Maximum Score on the Attitude towards Hygienic Condition Variables

i = 1. . . n = Number of Quality service variables included

In the present study, HCI is confined to less than 25, 25-50, 50-75 and 75-100 per cent. The distribution of patients according to the HCI is shown in Table 4.14.

Table 4.14 : The Hygenic Condition Index Among the Respondents

Sl. No.	HC Index (per cent)	Number of Respondents				Total
		Govt. Maternity and paediatric	Govt. Ortho. and general medicine	Private Maternity and paediatric	Govt. Ortho and general medicine	
1	Less than 25	—	—	—	—	—
2	25-50	—	—	—	4 (3.3)	4 (1)
3	50-75	40 (50)	68 (57)	16 (20)	60 (50)	184 (46)
4	75-100	40 (50)	52 (43)	64 (80)	56 (46.7)	212 (53)
	Total	**80 (100)**	**120 (100)**	**80 (100)**	**120 (100)**	**400 (100)**

* Figures within the parentheses denote the percentage

Totally, a maximum of 53 per cent of the patients have HCI of 75-100 per cent followed by 46 per cent who have HCI of 50-75 per cent. The number of patients who have HCI of 25-50 per cent constitutes 1 per cent of the total. Among the patients who have HCI of 50-75 per cent, the number of patients of the Government maternity and paediatric hospitals constitute 50 per cent whereas among the private maternity and paediatric patients, it constitutes 20 per cent. At the same, the number of patients of Government maternity having HCI of 75-100 per cent constitute 50 per cent to its total and among the patients of the private maternity and paediatric hospitals it constitutes 80 per cent. As regards hygienic conditions are concerned, it reveals that the patients of Government hospitals have poor attitude and there is an existence of better attitude among the patients of the private hospitals.

THE ATTITUDE OF THE PATIENTS TOWARDS HOSPITALITY

The attitudes of the patients is analysed with the help of the mean score on the six factors among the patients. For that purpose, the mean scores on six factors are calculated from the score of the respective variables in it among the four groups of the patients separately. In order to find out whether there is any significant difference among the four groups of the patients regarding their attitude towards six factors in hospitality, the one way analysis of the variance has been administered. The resultant mean score of the factors and the respective 'F' statistics are presented in Table 4.15.

Table 4.15 : The Attitude of the Respondents Towards Hospitality

Sl. No.	Hospitality	Mean score				F-Statistics
		Govt. Maternity and paediatric	Govt. Ortho. and general medicine	Private Maternity and paediatric	Private Ortho. and general medicine	
1.	The nursing assistants are courteous	4.150	3.667	4.400	3.167	15.33*
2.	All the personnel of the hospital are patient-friendly	3.500	3.367	4.250	4.133	36.77*
3.	The doctors in the hospital are very humane	4.050	3.600	4.400	4.233	16.47*
4.	The stay in the hospital is very pleasant and comfortable	4.150	3.400	4.350	4.033	22.05*
5.	The hospitality of the hospital staff is pleasing	4.250	3.867	4.400	4.100	7.383*
6.	The patients could feel at home in the hospital	4.100	3.633	4.350	4.167	14.10*

Source: Primary Data
*Significant at one per cent level

The patients of the private maternity and paediatric hospitals perceived highly important on all aspects of hospitality than the patients of the private orthopaedic and general medicine hospitals and the patients of Government hospitals of both maternity and paediatric as well as orthopaedic and general medicine hospitals. Hence, the respective mean scores on all the six factors in hospitality are greater than the others. The factors perceived as high among the patients of the private maternity and paediatric are 'the nursing assistants are courteous', 'the doctors in the hospital are very humane' and 'the hospitality of the hospital is very good'. Hence, the respective mean scores of all the three factors are 4.400. Among the patients of the private orthopaedic and general medicine hospital, these factors are 'the doctors in the hospital are very humane' and 'the patients could feel at home in the hospital'. Hence, the respective mean scores are 4.233 and 4.167. Among the patients of the Government maternity and paediatric hospitals, factors such as 'the hospitality of the hospital is very good' and 'the nursing assistants are courteous' were highly perceived. The patients of the Government orthopaedic and general medicine hospitals perceived the factors 'all the personnel of the hospital are patient-friendly' and 'the stay in the hospital is very pleasant and comfortable' as low. Hence, the mean scores are 3.367 and 3.400 respectively. The significant difference among the four groups of patients is identified regarding the perception on the hospitality in 'all the personnel of the hospital are patient-friendly', 'the stay in the hospital is very pleasant and comfortable' and 'the nursing assistants are courteous'. Hence, the respective 'F' statistics are significant at 1 per cent level. The analysis infers that the patients of the Government orthopaedic and general medicine hospital are poor in their perception of hospitality when compared to the other three groups of patients.

The Attitude towards Hospitality Index (HI) among the Respondents

The HI has been prepared for further analysis. The Hospitality index is calculated by

$$HI = \frac{\sum_{i=1}^{n} SAHVi}{\sum_{i=1}^{n} MSAHVi} \times 100$$

Where,

HI = Hospitality Index

SAHV = Score on the Attitude towards Hospitality Variables

MSAHV = Maximum Score on the Attitude towards Hospitality Variables

i = 1. . . n = Number of Hospitality variables included

In the present study, HI is confined to less than 25, 25-50, 50-75 and 75-100 per cent. The distribution of the patients according to the HI is shown in Table 4.16.

Table 4.16 : The Hospitality Index Among the Respondents

Sl. No.	HI (per cent)	Number of Respondents				
		Govt. Maternity and paediatric	Govt. Ortho. and general medicine	Private Maternity and paediatric	Govt. Ortho and general medicine	Total
1.	Less than 25	—	—	—	—	—
2.	25-50	—	—	—	—	—
3.	50-75	16 (20)	84 (70)	12 (15)	24 (20)	136 (34)
4.	75-100	64 (80)	36 (30)	68 (85)	96 (80)	264 (66)
	Total	**80 (100)**	**120 (100)**	**80 (100)**	**120 (100)**	**400 (100)**

* Figures within the parentheses denote the percentage

Totally, a maximum of 66 per cent of the patients have HI of 75-100 per cent followed by 34 per cent who have HI of 50-75 per cent. No patient of both the sectors namely public and private belongs to categories of HI of less than 25 per cent and 25-50 per cent. Among the patients of the maternity and paediatric hospitals who have HI of 75-100 per cent, the number of patients of the Government maternity and paediatric constitutes 80 percentage of its total whereas among the patients of private hospitals, it constitutes 85 percentage of the total. And, among the patients of orthopaedic and general medicine hospitals who have HI of 75-100 per cent, the number of patients of the Government hospital constitutes 30 percentage whereas among the patients of the private orthopaedic and general medicine hospitals, it constitutes 80 percentage of its total. It reveals the lower level of HI of the Government hospital patients when compared to the HI of the patients of the private hospitals.

THE ATTITUDE OF THE PATIENTS TOWARDS PHYSICAL EVIDENCE OF HEALTH SERVICE

The attitude of the patients is analysed with the help of the mean scores on the six factors among the patients. For that purpose, the mean scores on six factors are calculated from the score of the respective variables in it among the four groups of patients separately. In order to find out whether there is any significant difference among the four groups of patients regarding their attitude towards six factors in 'physical evidence of health service', the one way analysis of variance has been administered. The resultant mean score of the factors and the respective 'F' statistics are presented in Table 4.17.

The patients of the private maternity and paediatric hospitals perceived the four aspects of the physical evidence of health service more than the other three groups of the patients. The highly perceived factors among the patients of the private maternity and paediatric hospitals are 'patient - friendly messages are given by the service provider', 'there is a provision for remote encounter' 'the hospitals is an ISO certified institution' and 'the hospital provides tangible

Table 4.17 : The Attitude of the Respondents Towards Physical Evidence of Health Service

Sl. No.	Physical Evidence of Health Service	Mean score				F-Statistics
		Govt. Maternity and paediatric	Govt. Ortho. and general medicine	Private Maternity and paediatric	Private Ortho. and general medicine	
1.	The atmosphere of the hospital brings good and positive state of mind	4.900	3.800	4.500	4.367	39.03 *
2.	The hospital uses various means win the confidence of customers	3.800	3.400	3.900	3.933	10.03 *
3.	The hospital provides tangible evidence to show that service has been duly delivered	3.150	3.033	3.450	3.300	9.64 *
4.	There is a provision for remote encounter i.e. coming together of the patient and the service provider without actual physical contact	3.150	2.933	3.750	3.733	29.74 *
5.	Patient friendly messages are given by the service provider to improve understanding of the patients how to enjoy the best service.	4.000	3.233	4.200	4.066	38.01 *
6.	The hospital is an ISO certified institution	3.150	2.933	3.700	3.367	23.05 *

Source: Primary Data
*Significant at one per cent level

evidence' since the respective mean scores are 4.200, 3.750, 3.700 and 3.450 respectively. Among the patients of the Government maternity and paediatric hospitals, these factors are 'the atmosphere of the hospital brings good and positive state of mind' and 'patient-friendly messages are given by the service providers'. Hence, the respective mean scores are 4.900 and 4.000. The patients of the Government orthopaedic and general medicine perceived the factors like 'the hospital is an ISO certified institution' and 'the hospital provides tangible evidence' as low. Hence the mean scores are 2.932 and 3.033 respectively. The significant difference among the four groups of the patients is identified regarding the perception on the physical evidence of health service in 'the atmosphere of the hospital brings good and positive state of mind', 'patient-friendly messages are given by the service provider there is a provision for remote encounter since the respective 'F' statistic are significant at 1 per cent level. The analysis infers that the patients of Government hospitals are poor in their perception of the physical evidence of health service compared to the patients of the private hospitals.

The Attitude towards Physical Evidence of Health Service Index (PEHSI) among the Respondents

The PEHSI has been prepared for further analysis. The PEHSI is calculated by

$$\text{PEHSI} = \frac{\sum_{i=1}^{n} \text{SAPEHSVi}}{\sum_{i=1}^{n} \text{MSAPEHSVi}} \times 100$$

Where,

PEHSI = Physical Evidence Health Service Index

SAPEHSV = Score on the Attitude towards Physical Evidence Health Service Variables

MSAPEHSV = Maximum Score on the Attitude towards Physical Evidence Health Service Variables

i = 1. . . n = Number of Physical Evidence Health Service Variables.

In the present study, PEHSI is confined to less than 25, 25-50, 50-75 and 75-100 per cent. The distribution of patients according to the PEHSI is shown in Table 4.18.

Table 4.18 : The Hospitality Evidences of Health Services Index among the Respondents

Sl. No.	PEHS Index (per cent)	Number of Respondents				
		Govt. Maternity and paediatric	Govt. Ortho. and general medicine	Private Maternity and paediatric	Govt. Ortho and general medicine	Total
1	Less than 25	—	—	—	—	—
2	25-50	—	4 (3)	—	4 (3)	8 (2)
3	50-75	60 (75)	116 (97)	20 (25)	56 (47)	252 (63)
4	75-100	20 (25)	—	60 (75)	60 (50)	140 (35)
	Total	**80 (100)**	**120 (100)**	**80 (100)**	**120 (100)**	**400 (100)**

*Figures within the parentheses denote the percentage

Totally, a maximum of 63 percentage of the patients have PEHSI of 50-75 per cent followed by 35 percentage have PEHSI of 75-100 per cent. The number of patients who have PEHSI of 25-50 constitutes 2 percentage of the total. No patient has PEHSI of less than 25. Among the patients who have PEHSI of 50-75 per cent, the number of patients of the Government maternity and paediatric hospitals constitutes 75 percentage of its total whereas among the private hospitals, it constitutes 25 percentage. At the same time, among the patients who have PEHSI of 75 to 100 per cent, the number of Government maternity and paediatric hospitals constitutes 25 percentage whereas among the private hospitals, it constitutes 75 percentage of its total. It reveals the poor attitude towards physical evidence of health service found among the patients of the Government hospitals and better attitude among the patients of the private hospitals.

THE ATTITUDE OF THE PATIENTS TOWARDS INNOVATIVENESS

The attitude of the patients is anlaysed with the help of the mean score on the six factors among the patients. For that purpose, the mean scores on six factors are calculated from the score of respective variables in it among the four groups of patients exclusively. In order to find out whether there is any significant difference among the four groups of the patients regarding their attitude towards six factors in innovativeness, the one way analysis of variance has been administered. The resultant mean score of the factors and the respective 'F' statistics are presented in Table 4.19.

Table 4.19 : The Attitude of the Respondents Towards Innovativeness

Sl. No.	Innovativeness	Mean score				F-Statistics
		Govt. Maternity and paediatric	Govt. Ortho. and general medicine	Private Maternity and paediatric	Private Ortho. and general medicine	
1.	The hospital has all required innovative and sophisticated medical equipment	4.450	4.067	4.450	4.333	7.98*
2.	The doctors ensure the latest treatments	3.950	3.333	4.100	4.200	40.93*
3.	The creativity of the doctors in delivering health service is appreciatable	4.000	3.500	4.400	4.033	31.64*
4.	The pre-consultation system followed by the hospital is unique	3.800	3.300	4.050	4.366	49.81*
5.	The follow-up service provided by the hospital is unique	3.800	3.300	4.050	3.833	13.73*
6.	Patient relationship with management of the hospital is highly impressive	4.000	3.833	4.200	4.133	6.11*

Source: Primary Data
*Significant at one per cent level

The patients of the private maternity and paediatric hospitals perceived four aspects of innovativeness as highly favourable than the other three groups of patients. Hence, the respective mean scores on such factors in innovativeness are greater than others. The highly perceived factors among the patients of the private maternity and paediatric hospitals are 'the hospital has all required innovative and sophisticated medical equipment', 'the creativity of doctors in delivering health service is appreciatable', 'patient relationship management of the hospital' is highly unique and 'the doctors ensure latest treatments', since the respective mean scores are 4.450, 4.400, 4.200 and 4.100. Among the patients of the private orthopaedic and general medicine hospital, these factors are 'the pre-consultation system followed by the hospital is unique' and 'the hospital has all required innovative and sophisticated medical equipment'. Hence, the respective mean scores are 4.366 and 4.333. The patients of the Government maternity and paediatric hospitals perceived the factors like 'the hospital has all required innovative and sophisticated medical equipment' and 'patient relationship management of the hospital is highly unique' as high. Hence, the mean scores are 4.450 and 4.000 respectively. The patients of the Government orthopaedic and general medicine hospitals perceived the factors like 'the follow-up service provided by the hospital is highly unique', 'the doctors employ latest treatments' and 'the creativity of doctors in delivering health service is appreciatable' as very low. Hence, the respective mean scores are 3.300, 3.333 and 3.500. The significant difference among the four groups of the patients is identified regarding the perception on innovativeness in hospital marketing and they are: 'the pre-consultation system followed by the hospital is unique', 'the doctors ensure latest treatments' and 'the creativity of doctors in delivering health service is appreciatable'. Hence, the respective 'F' statistics are significant at 1 per cent level. The analysis infers that the patients of the Government hospitals are poor in their perception of the innovation in hospital marketing when compared to the perception of the patients of the private hospitals.

The Attitude towards Innovativeness Index (II) among the Respondents

The II has been prepared for further analysis. The Innovativeness index is calculated by

$$II = \frac{\sum_{i=1}^{n} SAIVi}{\sum_{i=1}^{n} MSAIVi} \times 100$$

Where,

II = Innovativeness Index

SAIV = Score on the Attitude towards Innovativeness Variables

MSAIV = Maximum Score on the Attitude towards Innovativeness Variables

i = 1. . . n = Number of Innovativeness Variables involved.

In the present study, II is confined to less than 25, 25-50, 50-75 and 75-100 per cent. The distribution of patients according to the II is shown in Table 4.20.

Table 4.20 : The Innovativeness Index Among the Respondents

Sl. No.	Innovativeness Index (per cent)	Number of Respondents				Total
		Govt. Maternity and paediatric	Govt. Ortho. and general medicine	Private Maternity and paediatric	Govt. Ortho and general medicine	
1.	Less than 25	—	—	—	—	—
2.	25-50	—	—	—	—	—
3.	50-75	24 (30)	104 (87)	4 (5)	28 (23)	160 (40)
4.	75-100	56 (70)	16 (13)	76 (95)	92 (77)	240 (60)
	Total	**80 (100)**	**120 (100)**	**80 (100)**	**120 (100)**	**400 (100)**

*Figures within the parentheses denote the percentage

Totally, a maximum of 60 percentage of the patients have II of 75-100 per cent followed by 40 percentage who have II of 50-75 per cent. No patient has II of both 25-50 per cent and less than 25 per cent. Among the patients of the maternity and childcare hospitals who have II of 50-75 per cent, the number of patients of the Government hospitals constitute 30 percentage to its total whereas among the patients of the private hospitals, it constitutes 5 percentage of the total. In the same time, among the patients of maternity and paediatric hospitals who have 75-100 per cent II, the number of patients of the Government hospitals constitutes 70 percentage whereas among the patients of private hospital, it constitutes 95 percentage. So also, in the case of the patients of the orthopaedic and general medicine hospital, the number of the Government hospital patients accounts for 13 percentage whereas among the patients of private hospitals, it accounts for 77 percentage. It reveals the poor attitude towards innovativeness found among the patients of the Government hospital and better attitude among the patients of private hospitals.

THE ATTITUDE OF PATIENTS TOWARDS FAMILIARITY OF THE HOSPITAL

The attitudes of the patients is analysed with the help of the mean score on the six factors among the patients. For that purpose, the mean scores on six factors are calculated from the score of the respective variables in it among the four groups of patients exclusively. In order to find out whether there is any significant difference among the four groups of patients regarding their attitude towards six factors in familiarity, the one way analysis of variance has been administered. The resultant mean score of the factors and the respective 'F' statistics are presented in Table 4.21.

The patients of the private orthopaedic and general medicine hospital perceived more highly on all aspects of familiarity than the other three groups of patients. Hence, the respective means score on all the six factors in familiarity

Table 4.21 : The Attitude of the Respondents Towards the Familiarity of the Hospital

Sl. No.	Familiarity	Mean score				F-Statistics
		Govt. Maternity and paediatric	Govt. Ortho. and general medicine	Private Maternity and paediatric	Private Ortho. and general medicine	
1	The doctors of the hospital are well known	1.600	1.700	2.150	2.500	17.37*
2	The nurses and other staff of the hospital are very familiar	1.450	1.100	1.450	2.033	27.81*
3	The doctors of the hospital are relatives	1.450	1.166	1.400	2.100	31.82*
4	The doctors of the hospital are friends	1.600	1.260	1.450	1.900	17.27*
5	The promoters of the hospitals are very familiar	1.350	1.266	1.500	1.933	21.29*
6	The doctors and other staff of the hospital are neighbours	1.400	1.466	1.700	1.733	7.36*

Source: Primary Data
* Significant at one per cent level

are greater than the others. The highly perceived factors among the private patients of orthopaedic and general medicine hospitals are 'the doctors of the hospital are well known', 'the doctors of the hospital are relatives', and 'the nurses and other staff of the hospital are very familiar'. Hence, the mean scores are 2.500, 2.100 and 2.033 respectively. Among the patients of the private maternity and paediatric hospitals these factors are 'the doctors of the hospital are well known', and 'the doctors and other staff of the hospital are neighbours'. Hence, the respective mean scores are 2.150 and 1.700. The patients of the Government maternity and paediatric hospitals as well as orthopaedic and general medicine hospitals perceived with regard to all the factors concerning familiarity aspect as low. The patients of the Government maternity and paediatric hospitals perceived the factors like 'the promoters of the hospitals are very familiar' and 'the doctors and other staff of the hospital are neighbours' as low. Hence, the mean scores are 1.350 and 1.400 respectively. Whereas in the case of the patients of the Government orthopaedic and general medicine hospital, these factors are 'the nurses and the other staff of the hospital are very familiar' and 'the doctors of the hospital are relatives. Hence, the respective mean scores are 1.100 and 1.166. The significant difference among the four groups of patients is identified depending upon the perception on familiarity in health services, like 'the doctors of the hospital are relatives', 'the nurses and other staff of the hospital are very familiar' and 'the promoters of the hospital are very familiar'. Hence, the respective 'F' statistics are significant at 1 per cent level. The analysis infers that the patients of the Government hospitals are poor in their perception of the familiarity in health services when compared to the patients of the private hospitals.

The Attitude towards Familiarity of the Hospital Index (FHI) among the Respondents

The FH index has been prepared for further analysis. The FH index is calculated by

$$\text{FHI} = \frac{\sum_{i=1}^{n} \text{SAFHVi}}{\sum_{i=1}^{n} \text{MSAFHVi}} \times 100$$

Where,

FHI = Familiarity of the Hospital Index

SAFHV = Score on the Attitude towards Familiarity of the Hospital Variables

MSAFHV = Maximum Score on the Attitude towards Familiarity of the Hospital Variables

i = 1. . . n = Number of Familiarity of the Hospital Variables involved.

In the present study, FHI is confined to less than 25, 25-50, 50-75 and 75-100 per cent. The distribution of patients according to the FHI is shown in Table 4.22.

Table 4.22 : The Familiarity of the Hospital Index Among the Respondents

Sl. No.	FH Index (per cent)	Number of Respondents				Total
		Govt. Maternity and paediatric	Govt. Ortho. and general medicine	Private Maternity and paediatric	Govt. Ortho and general medicine	
1.	Less than 25	20 (25)	32 (27)	24 (30)	20 (17)	96 (24)
2.	25-50	56 (70)	88 (73)	52 (65)	68 (57)	264 (66)
3.	50-75	4 (5)	—	4 (5)	28 (23)	36 (9)
4.	75-100	—	—	—	4 (3)	4 (1)
	Total	**80 (100)**	**120 (100)**	**80 (100)**	**120 (100)**	**400 (100)**

*Figures within the parentheses denote the percentage

Totally, a maximum of 66 percentage of the patients have FHI of 25-50 per cent followed by 24 percentage have FHI of less than 25 per cent. The number of patients who have FHI of 50-75 per cent constitutes 9 per cent of the total and the number of patients who have FHI of 75-100 per cent accounts for 1 per cent of the total. Among the patients of the Government maternity and paediatric hospitals, the number of patients who have FHI of 25-50 per cent constitutes 70 percentage of its total whereas among the patients of private maternity and paediatric hospital, it constitutes 65 percentage of its total. And, among the patients of the Government orthopaedic and general medicine hospitals, the number of patients who have FHI of 50-75 per cent constitutes 73 percentage whereas among the patients of the private hospitals, it constitutes 57 percentage of its total. It reveals the poor attitude towards familiarity found among the patients of private hospitals and better attitude among the patients of Government hospitals.

THE ATTITUDE LEVEL OF THE PATIENTS TOWARDS HOSPITAL SERVICE

In order to measure the level of attitude of the sample respondents towards the overall services provided by the hospitals in the study area, 12 components consisting of 72 explanatory statements were identified. The responses of sample respondents to each statement were measured with the help of Likert's five point scale, classified as five scores for "highly satisfied", four for "satisfied", three for "no answer", two for "not satisfied", and one for "highly not satisfied". After allotting scores for each component, the total scores of each respondent was computed.

On the basis of the total scores, arithmetic mean and standard deviations were computed for all the 400 sample respondents. Those who have scored above arithmetic mean plus standard deviation were categorised as high level, those who have scored below arithmetic mean minus standard deviation as low level and those with scores in between (Arithmetic mean + standard deviation) and (Arithmetic mean - standard derivation) were categorised as medium level. The following Table shows the classification of the respondents on the basis of level of attitude.

Table 4.23 : The Level of Attitude of the Sample Patient Respondents

Sl. No.	Level of attitude	Number of respondents	Percentage
1.	High level	88	22.0
2.	Medium level	238	59.5
3.	Low level	74	18.5
	Total	**400**	**100**

Source: Primary data

It is observed from Table 4.23 that out of 400 sample respondents, 88 (22.0 per cent) respondents had high level attitude, 238 (59.5 per cent) of them had medium level and 74 (18.5 per cent) of the respondents had low level attitude towards the service rendered by hospitals in Kanyakumari district.

FACTORS INFLUENCING THE ATTITUDE OF THE PATIENTS

There may be a number of factors influencing the level of attitude of the respondents on the over all service provided by hospitals in the study area. The independent variables such as age, gender, level of literacy, occupation, marital status, income, family size, area of residence and number of members in the family were considered for the purpose of analysis. By using Chi-square test an effort was made to find out whether such relationship was statistically significant.

The Age Group and Level of Attitude

There is a relationship between age and attitude. As people grow in age they tend to have different views and opinions over products and services. Age and attitude go hand-in-hand. As individuals are exposed to new and varied experiences through new environment and education by passage of time, change in their attitude is inevitable. Individuals of different age groups have different mindsets, aspirations, expectations, perceptions and accordingly different attitudes. In the present study, the relationship between the age of the respondents and their level of attitude towards the services provided by the hospitals has been duly analysed. The relevant results are presented in Table 4.24.

It is observed from Table 4.24 that out of 120 respondents belonging to the age group of 20-30 years, 36 (30 per cent), 68 (56.7 per cent) and 16 (13.3 per cent) have high, medium and low, level of attitude respectively. Of the 125 respondents who belong to the age group of 30-40 years, 24 (19.2 per cent), 76 (60.8 per cent) and 25 (20 per cent) possess a high, medium and low levels of attitude respectively. Among 80 respondents who belong to the age group of 40-50 years, 16 (20 per cent), 52 (65 per cent) and 12 (15 per cent) have a high, medium and low level of attitude respectively. Out of 75 respondents belonging to the age group of 50-60 years, 12 (16 per cent), 42 (56 per cent) and 21 (28 per cent) have high, medium and low levels of attitude respectively.

Table 4.24 : The Age Group of the Respondents and their Level of Attitude

Sl. No.	Age group	Level of attitude			Total
		High	Medium	Low	
1.	20 - 30	36 (30)	68 (56.7)	16 (13.3)	120 (100)
2.	30 - 40	24 (19.2)	76 (60.8)	25 (20)	125 (100)
3.	40 - 50	16 (20)	52 (65)	12 (15)	80 (100)
4.	50 - 60	12 (16)	42 (56)	21 (28)	75 (100)
	Total	**88 (22)**	**238 (59.5)**	**74 (18.5)**	**400 (100)**

Source: Primary Data
•Figures in parenthesis denote the percentage

It is also inferred from Table 4.24 that there is no apparent relationship between the age group of the respondents and their level of attitude to the services of hospitals in the study area.

In order to find out whether there is any significant relationship between age group and their level of attitude the null hypothesis that, "there exists no significant relationship between the age group and the level of attitude of the respondents towards the services rendered by the hospitals in Kanyakumari district" was framed and analysed with the help of Chi-square test. The result is presented in Table 4.25.

Table 4.25 : The Relationship Between age Group and Level of Attitude

Relation	x^2-value	Degrees of freedom	Table value of 5% significance
Age group and level of attitude	12.14*	6	12.6

Source: Computed from Table 4.24.
*Significance at 5 per cent level

It is observed from Table 4.25 that the calculated value x^2 (12.14) is smaller than its corresponding Table value (12.6) at 5 per cent level or significance. Therefore, the null hypothesis is accepted. Hence, it is concluded that there is no significant relationship between age group and the level of attitude of the sample patient respondents towards the service provided by hospitals in Kanyakumari district.

Gender and Level of Attitude

Due to biological differences between males and females there does exist noticeable difference in the attitude between them. This is true in the case of health care industry too. As the way in which male children are brought up is different from the way in which female children are brought up, there exists difference in their attitude towards services rendered by hospitals. Such differences in their attitude may be significant. In this study, the relationship between gender and level of attitude has been analysed and the necessary particulars are given in Table 4.26.

It is evident from Table 4.26 that out of 188 male respondents, 33 (17.5 per cent), 115 (61.2 per cent) and 40 (21.3 per cent) have a high, medium and low level of attitude respectively. Out of 212 female respondents, 55 (26 per cent), 123 (58 per cent) and 34 (16 per cent) respondents have high, medium and low level of attitude respectively.

Table 4.26 : The Gender of the Respondents and their Level of Attitude

Sl. No.	Gender	Level of attitude			Total
		High	Medium	Low	
1.	Male	33 (17.5)	115 (61.2)	40 (21.3)	188 (100)
2.	Female	55 (26)	123 (58)	34 (16)	212 (100)
	Total	**88 (22)**	**238 (59.5)**	**74 (18.5)**	**400 (100)**

Source: Primary Data
•Figures in parenthesis denote the percentage

It is also inferred from Table 4.26 that there is no apparent relationship between the gender and the level of attitude to the services of the hospitals in the study area.

In order to find out whether there is any significant relationship between the gender and level of attitude, the null hypothesis that, "There exists no significant relationship between Gender and the level of attitude of the respondents towards the services rendered by the hospitals in Kanyakumari district" was framed and analysed with the help of Chi-square test. The result is presented in Table 4.27.

Table 4.27 : The Relationship Between Gender and the Level of Attitude

Relation	x^2-value	Degrees of freedom	Table value of 5% significance
Gender and level of attitude	4.83*	2	5.99

Source: Computed from Table 4.26
* Significance at 5 per cent level

It is observed from Table 4.27 that the calculated value of x^2 (4.83 per cent) is smaller than its corresponding Table value

(5.99) at 5 per cent level of significance. Therefore, the null hypothesis is accepted. Hence, it is concluded that there exists no significant relationship between gender and the level of attitude of the sample respondents towards the services provided by hospitals in Kanyakumari District.

Literacy and Level of Attitude

It is said that there are three Es that affect an individual's attitude. They are Education, Environment and Experience. Thus, education or literacy plays an important role in influencing an individual's attitude. The literacy level of users of hospital services affects their level of attitude towards hospital marketing. As attitude is mainly formed by what type of education and what level of literacy one has, literacy has been identified and taken as an important variable affecting the attitude of the patients towards the services provided by the hospitals in the study area. The literacy level of the respondents and their level of attitude are shown in Table 4.28.

Table 4.28 : Literacy Level of the Respondents and Their Level of Attitude

Sl. No.	Literacy level	Level of attitude			Total
		High	Medium	Low	
1.	Illiterates	12 (16.7)	48 (66.7)	12 (16.6)	72 (100)
2.	Up to +2	36 (17.6)	114 (55.9)	54 (26.5)	204 (100)
3.	Graduates and post graduates	40 (32.3)	76 (61.3)	8 (6.5)	124 (100)
	Total	**88(22)**	**238(59.5)**	**74(18.5)**	**400(100)**

Source: Primary Data
•Figures in parenthesis denote the percentage

It is observed from Table 4.28 that out of 72 illiterate respondents, 12 (16.7 per cent), 48 (66.7 per cent) and 12 (16.6

per cent) have high, medium and low levels of attitude respectively. Of the 204 respondents of the literacy level up to +2, 36 (17.6 per cent), 114 (55.9 per cent) and 54 (26.5 per cent) respondents possess high, medium and low levels of attitude respectively. Among 124 respondents of graduates and post graduates, 40 (32.3 per cent), 76 (61.3 per cent) and 8 (6.5 per cent) have high, medium and low levels of attitude respectively.

It is inferred from Table 4.28 that there is no apparent relationship between the literacy level of the respondents and their level of attitude towards the services of the hospitals in the study area.

In order to find out whether there is any significant relationship between the literacy level of the patients and their level of attitude, the null hypothesis that, "there exists no significant relationship between the literacy level and the level of attitude of the respondents towards the services rendered by the hospitals in Kanyakumari District" was framed and analysed with the help of Chi-square test. The result is presented in Table 4.29.

Table 4.29 : The Relationship Between Literacy Level and Level of Attitude

Relation	x^2-value	Degrees of freedom	Table value of 5% significance
Literacy level and level of attitude	26.62*	4	9.49

Source: Computed from Table 4.28
* Significance at 5 per cent level

It is observed from the Table 4.29 that the calculated value of x^2 (26.62) is greater than its corresponding Table value (9.49) at 5 per cent level of significance. Therefore, the null hypothesis is rejected. Hence, it is concluded that there exists significant relationship between the literacy level and the level of attitude of the sample patient respondents towards the service provided by the hospitals in Kanyakumari district.

Occupations and Level of Attitude

Occupational status of individuals has a say over their attitude towards any product or service. Attitudes are expected to change as a function of experience. Different individuals receive different experiences based on their occupational status. Thus, eventually the attitude of the patients towards the hospital service is expected to change according to the type and nature of experience which they receive from their work places and through their colleagues. In this present study, the association between the occupational status of the patient respondents and their level of attitude towards hospital services has been analysed and the relevant results are shown in the Table 4.30.

Table 4.30 : The Occupation of Respondents and their Level of Attitude

Sl. No.	Occupation	Level of attitude			Total
		High	Medium	Low	
1.	Daily wage earners	10 (12.2)	54 (65.8)	18 (22)	82 (100)
2.	Agriculturalists	34 (22.7)	72 (48)	44 (29.3)	150 (100)
3.	Businessmen	44 (26.2)	112 (66.7)	12 (7.1)	168 (100)
	Total	**88 (22)**	**238 (59.5)**	**74 (18.5)**	**400 (100)**

Source: Primary Data
•Figures in parenthesis denote the percentage

It is observed from Table 4.30 that out of 82 respondents who are daily wage earners, 10 (12.2 per cent), 54 (65.8 per cent) and 18 (22 per cent) have high, medium and low levels of attitude respectively. Among the 150 respondents who are agriculturalists, 34 (22.7 per cent) 72 (48 per cent) and 44 (29.3

per cent) have high, medium and low levels of attitude respectively. Among 168 respondents who are businessmen and professionals 44 (26.2 per cent), 112 (66.7 per cent) and 12 (7.1 per cent) have high, medium and low levels of attitude respectively.

Table 4.30 also explains that there is no apparent relationship between the occupation of the respondents and their level of attitude to the services of the hospitals in the study area.

In order to find out whether there is any significant relationship between the occupation and the level of attitude the null hypothesis that, "there exists no significant relationship between the occupation and the level of attitude of the respondents towards services rendered by the hospitals ion Kanyakumari district" was framed and analysed with the help of Chi-square test. The result is presented in Table 4.31.

Table 4.31 : The Relationship Between Occupational Status and Level of Attitude

Relation	x^2-value	Degrees of freedom	Table value of 5% significance
Occupation and level of attitude	32.05*	4	9.49

Source: Computed from Table 4.30
* Significance at 5 per cent level

The computed value of x^2 (32.05) is greater than the corresponding Table value (9.49) at 5 per cent level of significance. Therefore, the null hypothesis is rejected. Hence, it is concluded that there exists significant relationship between occupational status and the level of attitude of the patient sample respondents towards the services provided by hospitals in Kanyakumari district.

Marital Status and the Level of Attitude

The way in which unmarried patients act or behave towards hospital services may be different from the way in which married patients behave. It is true that no two people behave in the same way. And, even the same person will not behave in the same way every time and under all occasions. The level of attitude of individuals does vary chiefly according to their marital status. This is true with the patients in availing health care services. Therefore, in the present study, the relationship between the marital status of the respondents and their level of attitude towards services provided by the hospitals in Kanyakumari district was analysed and the results are shown in Table 4.32.

Table 4.32 : The Marital Status of Respondents and Their Level of Attitude

Sl. No.	Marital status	Level of attitude			Total
		High	Medium	Low	
1.	Married	72 (20.9)	210 (61.1)	62 (18)	344 (100)
2.	Unmarried	16 (28.6)	28 (50)	12 (21.4)	56 (100)
	Total	**88 (22)**	**238 (59.5)**	**74 (18.5)**	**400 (100)**

Source: Primary Data
•Figures in parentheses denote percentage

It is observed from Table 4.32 that out of 344 married respondents, 72 (20.9 per cent), 210 (61.1 per cent) and 62 (18 per cent) of the respondents have high, medium and low levels of attitude respectively. Of the 56 respondents who are unmarried 16 (28.6 per cent), 28 (50 per cent) and 12 (21.4 per cent) of the respondents have high, medium and low levels of attitudes.

It is also inferred from Table 4.32 that there is no apparent relationship between marital status of the respondents and their level of attitude to the services of the hospitals in the study area.

In order to find out whether there is any significant relationship between marital status and the level of attitude the null hypothesis that "there exists no significant relationship between the marital status and the level of attitude of the respondents towards services rendered by the hospitals in Kanyakumari district" was framed and analysed with the help of Chi-square test. The result is presented in Table 4.33.

Table 4.33 : The Relationship Between Marital Status and the Level of Attitude

Relation	x^2-value	Degrees of freedom	Table value of 5% significance
Marital status and the level of attitude	2.568*	2	5.99

Source: Computed from Table 4.32
* Significance at 5 per cent level

It is observed from the Table 4.33 that the calculated value of x^2 (2.568) is smaller than its corresponding Table value (5.9) at 5 per cent level of significance. Therefore, the null hypothesis is accepted. Hence, it is concluded that there exists no significant relationship between marital status and the level of attitude of the sample patient respondents towards the services provided by the hospitals in Kanyakumari district.

Family Income and Level of Attitude

The attitude of the haves and the have-nots does differ from each other. No service is available free of cost. The attitude of the patients availing healthcare services is no exemption. The patients are expected to pay the due cost in the process of availing health services and getting cured of their physical ailments. The monthly family income of the respondents plays an important role in forming an attitude about services provided by the private as well as the Government hospitals. Hence, in this present study, the relationship between the monthly income of the family of the respondents and their level of attitude has been taken into account. The relevant information is shown in Table 4.34.

Table 4.34 : The Family Income of the Respondents and the Level of Their Attitude

Sl. No.	Family Income (Rs/month)	Level of attitude High	Medium	Low	Total
1.	Up to 5,000	48 (22.9)	111 (52.9)	51 (24.2)	210 (100)
2.	5,000 - 10,000	20 (17.9)	80 (71.4)	12 (10.7)	112 (100)
3.	Above 10,000	20 (25.6)	47 (60.3)	11 (14.1)	78 (100)
	Total	**88** **(22)**	**238** **(59.5)**	**74** **(18.5)**	**400** **(100)**

Source: Primary Data
•Figures in parentheses denote the percentage

Table 4.34 exhibits that out of 210 respondents whose monthly family income is up to Rs. 5000, 48 (22.9 per cent), 111 (52.9 per cent) and 51 (24.2 per cent) respondents have high, medium and low levels of attitude respectively. Of the 112 respondents whose family income is between Rs. 5000 and 10000, 20 (17.9 per cent), 80 (71.4 per cent) and 12 (10.7 per cent) respondents have high, medium and low levels of attitude respectively. Among 78 respondents whose family income is above Rs. 10,000, 20 (25.6 per cent), 47 (60.3 per cent) 11 (14.1 per cent) respondents have high, medium and low levels of attitude respectively.

It is inferred from Table 4.34 that there is no apparent relationship between the family income of the respondents and their level of attitude to the services of the hospitals in the study area.

In order to find out whether there is any significant relationship between family income and their level of attitude the null hypothesis that, "there exists no significant relationship between the family income and the level of attitude of the respondents towards the services rendered by the hospitals in Kanyakumari district" was framed and analysed with the help of Chi-square test. The result is presented in Table 4.35.

Table 4.35 : The Relationship Between Family Income and Level of Attitude

Relation	x^2-value	Degrees of freedom	Table value of 5% significance
Family income and level of attitude	13.94*	41	9.49

Source: Computed from Table 4.34
* Significance at 5 per cent level

The computed value of x^2 (13.94) is greater than its corresponding Table value (9.49) at 5 per cent level of significance. Therefore the null hypothesis is rejected. Hence, it is concluded that there exists significant relationship between family income and the level of attitude of the sample patient respondents towards the services provided by the hospitals in Kanyakumari district.

Number of Members in the Family and Level of Attitude

The number of members in the family or the family size plays an important role in the formation of the attitude of the patient towards the services provided by the hospitals. The size of the family may be either small or large. Depending upon the size of the family of the respondents the decision that they arrive at in availing health services from private hospital and / or Government hospital may be differed. In the present study, the relationship between the number of members in the family and level of attitude of the patients has been analysed and the related particulars are presented in Table 4.36.

It is observed from Table 4.36 that out of 156 respondents whose number of family members is up to three, 44 (28.2 per cent), 91 (58.3 per cent) and 21 (13.5 per cent) have high, medium and low levels of attitude respectively. Of the 208 respondents whose number of family members is 4-5, 36 (17.3 per cent), 129 (62 per cent) and 43 (20.7 per cent) respondents posses high, medium and low levels of attitude respectively. Among 36 respondents whose family consists of above 5 members, 8 (22.2 per cent), 18 (50 per cent) and 10 (27.8 per cent) respondents have high, medium and low levels of attitude respectively.

Table 4.36 : The Number of Members in the Family and Level of Attitude

Sl. No.	Members in the family	Level of attitude High	Medium	Low	Total
1.	Up to 3	44 (28.2)	91 (58.3)	21 (13.5)	156 (100)
2.	4 - 5	36 (17.3)	129 (62)	43 (20.7)	208 (100)
3.	above 5	8 (22.2)	18 (50)	10 (27.8)	36 (100)
	Total	88 (22)	238 (59.5)	74 (18.5)	400 (100)

Source: Primary Data
•Figures in parentheses denote the percentage

It is inferred from Table 4.36 that there is no apparent relationship between the number of members in family of the respondents and their level of attitude to the services of hospitals in the study area.

In order to find out whether there is any significant relationship between the number of family members of the sample patient respondents and their level of attitude, the null hypothesis that "there exists no significant relationship between the number of members in the family and the level of attitude of the respondents towards the services rendered by the hospitals in Kanyakumari district" was framed and analysed with the help of Chi-square test. The result is presented in Table 4.37.

Table 4.37 : The Relationship Between the Number of Members in the Family and the Level of Attitude

Relation	x^2-value	Degrees of freedom	Table value of 5% significance
Number of members in the family and the level of attitude	9.96	4	9.49

Source: Computed from Table 4.36
* Significance at 5 per cent level

It is observed from the Table 4.37 that the calculated value of x^2 (9.96) is greater than its corresponding Table value (9.49) at 5 per cent level of significance. Therefore, the null hypothesis is rejected. Hence, it is concluded that there exists significant relationship between the number of members in family and the level of attitude of the sample respondents towards the services provided by the hospitals in Kanyakumari district.

The Area of Residence and Level of Attitude

Environment has been considered as one of the triple E_s affecting attitude. Thus, the area where the respondents do reside has been instrumental in the formation of such attitude. Attitudes are of positive, negative or neutral views. The view of the respondents towards the services provided by the hospitals may be either positive or negative or neutral. As the nature of environment that prevails in the rural area is different from that of the urban area, there may be a relationship between the area of residence of the respondents and their level of attitude. The relationship between area of the respondents residence and their level of attitude has been depicted in Table 4.38.

It is observed from Table 4.38 that out of 240 respondents residing in the rural area, 60 (25 per cent), 128 (53.3 per cent) and 52 (21.7 per cent) have high, medium and low levels of attitudes respectively. Among 160 respondents residing in the urban area 28 (17.5 per cent) 110 (68.8 per cent) and 22 (13.7 per cent) have high, medium and low level of attitudes respectively.

Table 4.38 : The Residential Area of the Respondents and Their Level of Attitude

Sl. No.	Area of Residence	Level of attitude High	Medium	Low	Total
1.	Rural	60 (25)	128 (53.3)	52 (21.7)	240 (100)
2.	Urban	28 (17.5)	110 (68.8)	22 (13.7)	160 (100)
	Total	**88 (22)**	**238 (59.5)**	**74 (18.5)**	**400 (100)**

Source: Primary Data
•Figures in parentheses denote the percentage

From Table 4.38, it is inferred that there is no apparent relationship between the area of residence and the level of attitude of the patient respondents to the services of the hospitals in the study area.

In order to find out whether there is any significant relationship between the area of residence and the level of attitude of the respondents, the null hypothesis that "There exists no significant relationship between the area of residence and the level of attitude of the respondents towards the services rendered by the hospitals in Kanyakumari district" was framed and analysed with the help of Chi-square test. The results are presented in Table 4.39.

It is observed from Table 4.39 that the calculated value of x^2 (26.62) is greater than its corresponding Table value (9.49) at 5 per cent level of significance. Therefore, the null hypothesis is rejected. Hence, it is concluded that there exists significant relationship between the area of residence and the level of attitude of the sample respondents towards the service provided by the hospitals in Kanyakumari district.

Table 4.39 : Relationship Between Area of Residence and Level of Attitude

Relation	x^2-value	Degrees of freedom	Table value of 5% significance
Area of residence and level of attitude	26.62*	4	9.49

Source: Computed from Table 4.38
* Significance at 5 per cent level

THE PROBLEMS FACED BY THE PATIENT RESPONDENTS

By and large, the patients somehow face problems in availing medical service from both the private as well as the Government hospitals.

The Problems Faced by Patients of the Private Hospitals

The following are a few identified problems that are being faced by patients of the private hospitals :

Poor pre-consultancy service : Pre-consultancy service plays an important role in availing healthcare service from the private hospitals. Pre-consultancy service includes fixing appointment with the doctors, receiving token to consult the doctor, receiving I.P chart, taking preliminary tests like temperature B.P. It is true that many patients become impatient if any improper and unfriendly pre-consultancy service is given to them.

High fees : No medical service is provided by the private hospitals free of cost. Fees are being charged from the patients by the private hospitals for the given treatment. Many a time, patients don't have affordability to meet the high cost of health care services. Further, for many patients, fee may become the single determinant in choosing a private hospital.

Discrimination in providing quality service : It is hard to see doctors who practice hundred per cent fairness in their dealings in general and in providing quality service in specific.

In many cases, the providers of private health service do discriminate their patients by family, region, familiarity and the like. Hence, this has been identified as one of the five problems of patients of private hospitals.

Long waiting time : Time is precious to every person. Very often patients are to wait for a long time to get treated and cured. It is explicit that patients murmuring during such cases and this may eventually cause them to move to other hospital.

Discrimination in fixing fees : No uniformity is maintained by the providers of private health services in fixing fees for providing medical treatments. The providers normally charge high from an unknown patient and at the same time, a comparative low fee from known patients. This discrimination in fixing fee becomes a constraint for the patient to avail quality health service.

The patients were asked to rank the identified problems. The order of merit assigned by the respondents were converted in to scores by using Garrett's Ranking Technique.[1] This method was suggested by Garrett for converting the rank into scores when number of items ranked different from respondent to respondent. The per cent position for each rank was found using the following formula:

$$\text{Per cent position} = \frac{100(R_{ij} - 0.5)}{N_j}$$

where

R_{ij} = Rank given to i^{th} factor by j^{th} individual

N_j = Number of factors ranked by j^{th} individual

By referring the table given by Garrett, the per cent position estimated were converted into scores. Then for each factor, the scores of various respondents were added and divided by the number of respondents to arrive at the mean score. The mean scores thus obtained for each factor were arranged in a descending order. The factor with highest mean score was given the first rank, followed by second, third and so on.

Table 4.40 : Patients' Problems in Availing Health Service from Private Hospitals

Sl. No.	Problem	Mean Score	Rank
1.	High fees	54.32	I
2.	Discrimination in providing quality service	49.28	II
3.	Poor pre-consultancy service	47.15	III
4.	Discrimination in fixing fees	42.93	IV
5.	Long waiting time	40.18	V

Source: Primary Data

Table 4.40 depicts the problems that are being faced by the patients of private hospitals along with their mean scores and ranks. It is inferred from Table 4.40 that of the five identified problems, the problem of 'high fees' is ranked as the first and foremost problem with the highest mean score of 54.32 followed by the 'problem of discrimination in providing quality service' with a mean score of 49.28. The problem 'poor pre-consultancy service' is ranked third with the mean score of 47.15 followed by 'discrimination in fixing fees' with a mean score of 42.93 and the last rank is given to 'long waiting time' with the least mean score of 40.18.

Problems Faced by Patients of Government Hospitals

The nature and the variety of problems that are being faced by the patients of Government hospitals may be different from that of the problems of the patients of private hospitals. The following problems have been identified:

No personal attention : It is said that no personal attention is given in Government hospitals. Further, there is no cordial relationship between the patients and the staff of Government hospitals. Thus, absence of personal attention has been considered as an important problem which is being faced by the patients of Government hospitals.

Inadequate staff for emergency : Inadequate manpower of all categories like doctors, nurses and other medical assistants is an important problem prevailing in Government hospitals. Patients of Government hospitals do face this particular problem every now and then.

Poor hygienic condition : The atmosphere which is prevailing within the premises of Government hospitals including PHCs and HSCs is not hygienic. Hence, most of the patient respondents of Government hospitals consider this as a major problem.

Poor quality of service : In general, the quality of medical service which is given by Government hospitals is considered to be inferior. Many reasons can be attributed for this.

Tips/Money demanded by sub-staff : To insure prompt service in Government hospitals, patients are expected to pay tips or some amount of money to the sub-staff of Government hospitals. Thus, this has become one of the major problems of the patients of Government hospitals.

To rank the identified problems of patients of Government hospitals, Garrett's Ranking Technique was used and the results are shown in Table 4.41.

Table 4.41 : Patients' Problems in Availing Health Service from Government Hospitals

Sl. No.	Problem	Mean Score	Rank
1.	No personal attention	58.37	I
2.	Poor quality of service	55.11	II
3.	Poor hygienic condition	51.17	III
4.	Inadequate staff for emergency	44.08	IV
5.	Tips/money demanded by sub-staff	41.30	V

Source: Primary Data

Table 4.41 clearly shows the problems of patients of Government hospitals along with their respective mean score and ranks. It is obvious from Table 4.41 that of the five identified problems, the problem of 'No personal attention' is ranked first with the highest mean score 58.37 followed by 'poor quality of service' with a mean score of 55.11. The problem of 'poor hygienic condition' has been rank third with a mean score of 51.17 followed by 'inadequate staff for emergency' with a mean score 44.08. The problem called 'tips/ money demanded by sub-staff' has been ranked as the last with the least mean score of 41.30.

SUMMARY

This chapter aimed at studying the attitude of the patient respondents towards various aspects of marketing of hospital services and the problems that have been faced by them in availing health services from the Government as well as the private hospitals. Eight independent variables which are influencing the attitude of the patients were identified by the researcher and Chi-square test was applied. Of the factors identified and tested factors like literacy level of the respondents, occupation, income, size of the family and area of residence were found to be significant. However, the factors like age, gender and marital status of the patient respondents have proved that there exists no significant relationship between the independent factors and the level of attitude towards the health services provided by the hospitals in Kanyakumari district. It was found from this part of the study that of the five identified problems, the problem of 'high fees' is ranked as the first and foremost problem by the patients of the private hospitals while the problem of 'No personal attention' is ranked as the first and foremost by the patients of the Government hospitals.

REFERENCES

1. Henery E. Garrett and woodworth, P.S. 1969. *Statistics in Psychology and Education* Vileas Fetter and Science Private Ltd. Bombay, p. 329.

CHAPTER 5

The Costs and Returns Analysis of Hospital Services

INTRODUCTION

This part of the study deals with the profile of sample hospitals both private and Government and also the cost of providing hospital services and the cost and return analysis of the service providers. Nevertheless, the cost and return analysis of the study is only confined to private healthcare providers since Government hospitals are public sector hospitals and not aiming at earning profit. In ascertaining the cost of hospital services the variable costs and the fixed costs have been duly taken into account. For the analysis of costs and returns of private hospitals, the hospitals providing general medicine have not been included as the average cost and return of such hospitals do vary very much from one another. This part of the study also includes the problems that are being encountered by both the service providers — providers of private healthcare services and the providers of public healthcare services.

PROFILE OF THE SAMPLE HOSPITALS

Like every individual, every institution has its own profile otherwise called characteristic features. The profile of the sample patient respondents is given in the second chapter of this study. In this part of the study, the profile of the sample hospitals is given.

The Age of the Hospitals

The age of the hospitals refers to the length of period of medical service from the year in which the hospital was established. A hospital's length of service may have its own influence over its performance. The age of the sample hospitals is given in Table 5.1.

Table 5.1 : Length of Service of Hospitals

Sl. No.	Length (in years)	Government Hospital		Private Hospital		Total
		Maternity and Paediatric	Orthopaedic and General Medicine	Maternity and Paediatric	Orthopaedic and General Medicine	
1.	Below 5 years	2 (11.8)	3 (17.6)	5 (29.4)	7 (41.2)	17 (100)
2.	5 - 10 years	4 (15.7)	6 (25.0)	6 (25.0)	8 (33.3)	24 (100)
3.	10 - 15 years	4 (26.2)	5 (33.8)	2 (13.8)	4 (26.2)	15 (100)
4.	15 - 20 years	7 (22.6)	12 (39.6)	5 (15.2)	7 (22.6)	31 (100)
5.	Above 20 years	3 (23.6)	4 (30.9)	2 (15.6)	4 (30.9)	13 (100)
	Total	**20 (20)**	**30 (30)**	**20 (20)**	**30 (30)**	**100 (100)**

Source: Primary data
•Figures in parentheses denote the percentage

Table 5.1 exhibits that out of the 100 sample hospitals, 31 hospitals (31 per cent) have 15-20 years of service in providing health service, 24 hospitals (24 per cent) have been providing medical service for the last 5-10 years, the length of service of 17 hospitals is below 5 years, the length of service of 15 hospitals falls between 10-15 years and 13 hospitals have above 20 years of length of service. Thus, it is inferred that the majority (59 per cent) of the sample hospitals have more than 10 years of service in providing medical service. It is also inferred that most of the private hospitals (52 per cent) have shorter length of service of below 5 years and 5-10 years.

Number of Beds

A hospital is known by many factors. However, an important factor with which a hospital is known for is by the number of beds that are found in the hospital. As a library is known by the number of books it contains, a hospital is also always known by the number of beds it has. The number of beds which are found in the sample hospitals is presented in Table 5.2.

Table 5.2 : Bed-wise Distribution of Sample Provider Respondents

Sl. No.	No. of Beds	Government Hospital		Private Hospital		Total
		Maternity and Paediatric	Orthopaedic and General Medicine	Maternity and Paediatric	Orthopaedic and General Medicine	
1.	Up to 10	10 (31.2)	14 (43.7)	5 (15.7)	3 (9.4)	32 (100)
2.	10 - 20	2 (11.1)	4 (22.2)	7 (38.9)	5 (27.8)	18 (100)
3.	20 - 30	4 (13.3)	6 (20)	6 (20)	14 (46.7)	30 (100)
4.	Above 30	4 (20)	6 (30)	2 (10)	8 (40)	20 (100)
	Total	**20 (20)**	**30 (30)**	**20 (20)**	**30 (30)**	**100 (100)**

Source: Primary data
•Figures in parentheses denote the percentage

It is evident from Table 5.2 that 32 hospitals (32 per cent) have beds up to 10, 18 hospitals (18 per cent) have beds between 10-20, more number of hospitals (30 per cent) have beds between 22-30 and among the 30 hospitals 20 are private hospitals. And 20 hospitals (20 per cent) have above 30 beds. Thus, it is inferred that the private hospitals have more number of beds (30 as against 20) than the public sector hospitals.

Types of Public and Private Sector Hospitals

In the case of public sector health establishments there are three types of establishments in this study area. They are: the Government hospitals, the Primary Health Centres (PHCs) and the Health Sub-Centres (HSCs). Likewise, in the case of the private health sector establishments, there are three types of establishments namely hospitals, nursing homes and clinics (though there are not much of characteristic differences among them). The classification of the sample Government healthcare establishments and the private health care establishments on the basis of their types are presented in Table 5.3 and 5.4 respectively.

Table 5.3 : Distribution of Public Sector Hospitals on the Basis of their Types

Sl. No.	Type	Government Hospital		Total
		Maternity and Paediatric	Orthopaedic and General Medicine	
1.	Government Hospital	4 (40)	6 (60)	10 (100)
2.	PHCs	12 (40)	18 (60)	30 (100)
3.	HSCs	4 (40)	6 (60)	10 (100)
	Total	**20** **(40)**	**30** **(60)**	**50** **(100)**

Source: Primary data

•Figures in parentheses denote the percentage

It is clear from Table 5.3 that out of the 50 sample public sector hospitals 10 belong to the category of hospitals, 30 to PHCs and 10 to HSCs. It is inferred that most of the public sector health institutions in the study are in the form of PHCs.

It is clear from Table 5.4 that out of the 50 sample private hospitals, 40 belong to the category of hospitals, seven to nursing homes and three to clinics. Thus, it is inferred that most of the private sector health establishments are in the form of hospitals.

Table 5.4 : Classification of Private Sector Hospitals on the Basis of their Types

Sl. No.	Type	Private Sector Health Establishment		Total
		Maternity and Paediatric	Orthopaedic and General Medicine	
1.	Hospitals	17 (42.5)	23 (57.5)	40 (100)
2.	Nursing Homes	2 (28.6)	5 (71.4)	7 (100)
3.	Clinics	1 (33.3)	2 (66.7)	3 (100)
	Total	**20 (40)**	**30 (60)**	**50 (100)**

Source: Primary data
•Figures in parentheses denote the percentage

The Existence of Marketing Department

It is being witnessed that many service organisations including educational institutions and healthcare organisations have started realising the importance of marketing and accordingly the importance of the existence of a marketing department in those organisations. Nevertheless, the person who is incharge of marketing may not be called and designated as marketing manager but as customer relations manager and/or as public relations officer. The details about the existence of the marketing department in the sample hospitals are given in Table 5.5.

It is evident from Table 5.5 that there is non-existence of marketing department in the entire sample Government hospitals. But, the marketing department exists only in four out of the 50 sample private hospitals. Thus, it is inferred that most of the sample private hospitals and all the sample Government hospitals do not have exclusive marketing departments.

Table 5.5 : The Existence of Marketing Department in the Sample Hospitals

Sl. No.	Existence of Marketing Department	Government Hospital		Private Hospital		Total
		Maternity and Paediatric	Orthopaedic and General Medicine	Maternity and Paediatric	Orthopaedic and General Medicine	
1.	Yes	—	—	1 (25)	3 (75)	4 (100)
2.	No	20 (20.8)	30 (31.2)	19 (19.8)	27 (28.2)	96 (100)
	Total	**20 (20)**	**30 (30)**	**20 (20)**	**30 (30)**	**100 (100)**

Source: Primary data
*Figures in parentheses denote the percentage

Capital Investment

Huge amount of capital has been invested by the providers of private healthcare service and every provider is still expected to invest adequately so as to meet the infrastructural facilities and install modern equipment and thereby fulfil the demands of the patients. The particulars of the capital investment of the providers of the private health sector are shown in Table 5.6.

Table 5.6 clearly exhibits the amount of capital that has been invested by the providers of private maternity, paediatric and orthopaedic medical services. It is obvious from Table 5.6 that orthopaedic private hospitals invested much more than the private maternity, paediatric and general medicine hospitals. Out of the 50 sample private hospitals providing maternity, paediatric, Orthopaedic and general medicine hospital / medical services, only nine hospitals have invested above Rs. 1 crore and it is significant to note that of the nine, seven are Orthopaedic hospitals. Thus, it is inferred that the Orthopaedic private hospitals have invested much more than that of the private maternity, paediatric and general medicine hospitals.

Table 5.6 : Capital Investments by the Providers of

Private Health Service

No.	(in Rs.)	Maternity	Paediatric	Orthopaedic	General Medicine	
1.	Up to 20 lakhs	1 (16.7)	2 (33.3)		3 (50)	6 (100)
2.	20 - 60 lakhs	8 (33.3)	7 (29.2)	3 (12.5)	6 (25.0)	24 (100)
3.	61 - 100 lakhs	1 (9.1)	1 (9.1)	5 (45.4)	4 (36.4)	11 (100)
4.	Above 1 crore	—	—	7 (77.8)	2 (22.2)	9 (100)
	Total	**10** **(20)**	**10** **(20)**	**15** **(30)**	**15** **(30)**	**50** **(100)**

Source: Primary data
•Figures in parentheses denote the percentage

THE COSTS AND RETURNS ANALYSIS OF HOSPITAL SERVICES

In the process of providing healthcare services, the providers incur costs both variable and fixed. Variable costs such as medicines supplied, payment of fees for visiting consultants, laboratory costs and laundry charges vary based on the volume of health services provided or based on the number of patients treated. Fixed costs such as administrative overheads including payment of salaries to the personnel of the hospitals, rental value of hospital land and building, service and other taxes and other fixed costs like depreciation, insurance premium, interest on capital are being intact and constant irrespective of the volume of service provided and number of patients treated.

Fixed Costs

Fixed costs are considered to be the elements of cost which do not vary with the volume of production. It is based on the presumption that the installed production capacity is fixed and finalised. These costs are required to be incurred regardless of the level of output and sales. Depreciation, Property taxes, Interest, Insurance premium, Rent, supervisory and management salaries are typical examples of fixed costs. In hospital management, the use of various equipment, devices, apparatus and machines are inevitable and therefore, the depreciation cost is found important.[1] Hospitals or healthcare organisations taking loans or borrowing from banks or financial institutions have to pay interest. The hospital staff are paid and thus fixed cost becomes relevant while speaking the cost of private health services.

Variable Costs

Variable costs are those which vary directly with the actual volume of production or sale. This makes it clear that the variable cost per unit of output is found to be constant and with a change in the output, there is a proportionate change in the total variable costs. Variable costs are also called direct costs. In the case of private hospitals, cost of medicine, payment of fees to visiting doctors and the like are considered as variable cost.

Returns

It means the amount of fees or charges that have been collected from the patients by the providers for the given medical treatment minus the total costs incurred in providing such medical treatment.

The Cost Per Patient Day and the Costs and Returns Analysis of Private Hospital Services

In analysing the cost of hospital services, cost per patient day of private hospital services has been arrived at as follows:

$$\text{Cost per patient day} = \frac{\text{*Total cost per year}}{\text{**Total number of patient days}} \quad 2$$

* Total variable cost + Total fixed cost per year

** Number of beds × average number of days occupied in a month × 12

The cost and return analysis has been done in the following manner:

$$\text{Profit per patient day} = \frac{\text{Profit per annum}}{\text{Number of patient days per year}}$$

$$\text{Profit-Volume ratio} = \frac{\text{Contribution}}{\text{Total revenue}} \times 100$$

The cost per patient day of providing private maternity service in the study area is presented in Table 5.7.

Table 5.7 : Cost Per Patient Day of Private Maternity Health Service in Kanyakumari District

		Rs./p.a.	Rs./p.a.	Rs./p.a.	to total
	Visiting doctors fees	1,70,300	8,35,200	10,05,500	14.14
	Laboratory cost	1,35,600	5,91,600	7,27,200	10.14
	Laundry charges for bed linen	30,500	1,04,400	1,34,900	1.72
	Total variable cost	7,62,400	37,93,200	45,55,600	65.10
2.	**Fixed cost:**				
	Administrative over-heads			5,76,420	8.24
	Rental value of land and building			2,40,000	3.43
	Service and other taxes			3,86,040	5.51
	Other fixed costs including depreciation			12,39,804	17.72
	Total fixed cost			24,42,264	34.90
3.	**Total cost (1 + 2)**			**69,97,864**	**100**
4.	Number of patient days			3,960	
5.	Cost per patient day			1,767.14	

Source: Primary Data

Table 5.7 clearly depicts the variable cost, the fixed cost and the total cost incurred in providing private maternity service. It is clear from Table 5.7 that of the total costs, the share of the variable cost is 65.10 per cent whereas the share of fixed costs to total costs is 34.90 per cent. Thus, it is inferred that the share of variable costs to total costs is greater than that of the share of fixed costs to total costs in providing private maternity service. Among the variable costs, medicines supplied that is costs of medicines constitutes 39.10 per cent of the total costs of private maternity service. Among the fixed costs, the proportion of other fixed costs including deprecation constitutes 17.72 per cent of the total costs. It is also inferred from Table 5.7 that the cost per patient day of private maternity health service amounts to Rs. 1767.14.

The costs and returns analysis of the private maternity service is depicted in Table 5.8.

Table 5.8 : The Costs and Returns Analysis of Private Maternity Hospitals in Kanyakumari District

1.	[illegible]	[illegible]
	Caesarean delivery	[illegible]
2.	**Total revenue**	**96,51,000**
3.	Less variable cost	45,55,600
4.	**Contribution**	**50,95,400**
5.	Less fixed cost	24,42,264
6.	**Profit**	**26,53,136**
7.	No. of patient days	3,960
8.	Profit per patient day	**669.98**
9.	**Profit - volume ratio (in percentage)**	**52.79**

Source: Primary Data

Table 5.8 exhibits cost and return analysis of private maternity hospitals. It is evident from Table 5.8 that there is an annual contribution of Rs. 50,95,400/- and after meeting annual fixed cost of Rs. 24,42,264, there is an annual profit of Rs. 26,53,136. The profit per patient day is Rs. 669.98. It is also inferred from the table that the P/V ratio is 52.79 per cent.

The total cost per patient day of paediatric service in Kanyakumari District is presented in Table 5.9.

Table 5.9 : The Cost Per Patient Day of Paediatric Services in Kanyakumari District

1.	**Variable cost:**		
	Medicines supplied	4,60,800	19.26
	Laundry charges for bed linen	1,44,000	5.70
	Total variable cost	**13,72,800**	**55.02**
2.	**Fixed cost:**		
	Administrative overheads	3,88,560	15.57
	Rental value of land and building	1,80,000	7.31
	Service and other taxes	1,40,160	5.52
	Other fixed costs including depreciation	4,13,750	16.58
	Total fixed cost	**11,22,470**	**44.98**
3.	**Total cost**	**24,95,270**	**100**
4.	Number of patient days	5,760	
5.	Cost per patient day	433.21	

Source: Primary Data

It is observed from Table 5.9 that of the total annual cost of Rs. 24,95,270, Rs. 13,72,800 (55.02 per cent) is represented by total variable costs and the ratio of fixed costs to the total costs is 44.98 per cent. Among the variable costs, it is the cost of medicine which has the highest proportion of 19.62 per cent of the total costs and the second highest variable costs is the laboratory cost which constitutes 19.02 per cent of the total costs. Among the fixed costs, the proportion of other fixed costs stands first with 16.58 per cent to the total costs of providing paediatric service. It is also inferred that the cost per patient day is Rs. 433.21. Thus, it is inferred that the share of the variable costs to the total costs for providing paediatric service is higher than the share of fixed costs to the total costs.

The profit per patient day of paediatric hospitals in Kanyakumari district is presented in Table 5.10.

Table 5.10 : The Costs and Returns Analysis of Private Paediatric Hospitals in Kanyakumari District

1.	**Total revenue**	**35,04,000**
2.	Less variable cost	13,72,800
3.	**Contribution**	**21,31,200**
[illegible]	[illegible]	[illegible]
5.	**Profit**	**10,08,730**
6.	No. of patient days	57,60
7.	**Profit per patient day**	**175.13**
8.	**Profit-volume ratio (in percentage)**	**60.82**

Source: Primary Data

It is evident from Table 5.10 that there is an annual profit of Rs. 10,08,730/- in providing paediatric medical service to patients. Further, it is observed that there is a profit per patient day of Rs. 175.13. It is also observed that the profit volume ratio of the sample paediatric hospitals is 60.82 per cent.

The component cost as well as the total cost per patient day for private Orthopaedic service in Kanyakumari district are given in Table 5.11.

Table 5.11 reveals the component and the total variable costs, component and the total fixed costs and also the total costs of providing Orthopaedic service by private hospitals. The share of the total annual variable costs is 77.18 per cent towards the total annual costs of Rs. 5,03,28,297 while the proportion of the total fixed costs is just 22.82 per cent.

Table 5.11 : The Cost Per Patient Day of Private Orthopaedic Service in Kanyakumari District

1. **Variable cost:**				
Medicines supplied	1,01,75,860	1,27,79,604	2,29,55,364	45.26
Laundry charges for bed linen	1,22,400	78,300	2,00,700	0.40
Total variable cost	1,79,30,260	2,09,14,452	3,88,44,612	77.18
2. **Fixed cost:**				
Administrative over heads			11,44,800	2.27
Rental value of land and building			3,00,000	0.60
Service and other taxes			25,25,760	5.01
Other fixed costs including depreciation			75,13,125	14.94
Total fixed cost			**1,14,83,685**	**22.82**
3. **Total cost (1 + 2)**			**5,03,28,297**	**100**
4. Number of patient days			11,856	
5. **Cost per patient day**			**4,244.96**	

Source: Primary Data

Significantly share of the total annual variable costs towards the total annual costs is much greater than that of the share of the total fixed costs. Among the variable costs, the proportion of the costs of medicines is 45.26 per cent to the total annual costs of providing orthopaedic service. Thus, it is inferred that by exercising an effective control over the variable costs in general and over the costs of medicines in specific, Orthopaedic hospitals could cut down its total costs to a considerable extent. Further, it is also observed from Table 5.11 that among the various fixed costs it is other fixed costs which have a very high share of 14.94 per cent towards the total annual costs for providing Orthopaedic service. And, the cost per patient day of orthopaedic service amounts to Rs. 4244.96.

The costs and returns analysis of private Orthopaedic hospitals in Kanyakumari district is presented in Table 5.12.

Table 5.12 : The Costs and Returns Analysis of the Private

Orthopaedic Hospitals in Kanyakumari District

1.	Revenue from Orthopaedic services:	
	Single fracture	2,76,48,000
	Multi fracture	3,54,96,000
2.	Total revenue	6,31,44,000
[illegible]	[illegible]	[illegible]
4.	Contribution	2,42,99,388
5.	Less fixed cost	1,14,83,685
6.	**Profit**	**1,28,15,703**
7.	No. of patient days	11,856
8.	**Profit per patient day**	**1,080.95**
9.	Profit-volume ratio (in percentage)	38.48

Source: Primary Data

It is evident from Table 5.12 that there is an annual total profit of Rs. 12815703 in providing orthopaedic medical services by the private hospitals. Further, it is also evident that the amount of profit patient per day is Rs. 1080.95. Thus, it is inferred from the table that the profit of the private orthopaedic hospitals in average is fair and sound. It is also evident from Table 5.12 that the p/v ratio of the private orthopaedic hospitals is 38.48 per cent.

PROBLEMS ENCOUNTERED BY THE PROVIDERS OF HEALTH SERVICES

Delivering quality health services at the right time, in the right manner, at the right place, to the right patients, and at a fair price may not be an easy task. It involves a lot of problems and constraints on the part of the providers. It is true that both the providers of the private health service as well as the providers of the public health service in general are facing a lot of problems in providing health services to the patients.

The Problems Encountered by the Providers of Private Health Service

The following are some of the major identified problems that are being encountered by the providers of the private health services. They are: presence of stiff competition, high rate of staff turnover, easy availability of alternative medical treatments, the complaining and agitating attitude of the patients and the problem of maintaining trade-off between quality and cost. The provider respondents were asked to give their response over those identified problems and they were also asked to rank those problems according to their level of importance. By using Garrett's Ranking Technique, the first most and the second most important problems and so on were determined.

The presence of stiff competition : Today's business world is rightly described as highly competitive. Even in the service sector, stiff competition does prevail. This is genuine especially in the case of healthcare industry due to the mushroom growth of the private hospitals. Subsequently, every provider of the private health sector has to strive to succeed and to survive in the remarkably competitive health care industry.

The high rate of the staff turnover : Most of the private hospitals have the problem of retaining their trained staff in their respective hospitals for a longer period. This is usually for various reasons such as the high expectation of the staff regarding salary and their aspiration towards better jobs. When adequately trained staff move from one hospital to another hospital, the hospital loses not only a trained staff but also the confidence of the patients towards hospital services.

Easy availability of alternative medical treatments : The doctors and the providers of private allopathic medical service do face an important problem by name 'easy availability of alternative medical treatments' like ayurveda, siddha, homoeopathy. Especially in Kanyakumari district the intensity of the problem is still very high.

The complaining and agitating attitude of the patients: It is normally challenging to please any customer and it is still more challenging to please patients in a hospital. When the providers are unable to fulfil the expectations of the patients and fail to ensure speedy recovery from their physical ailments, they complain and they also get agitated. Such complains and agitations generally hamper the profession of the providers.

The problem of maintaining trade-off between quality and cost : Maintaining trade-off between profitability and liquidity is the most critical job of a financial manager. In the case of hospital marketing, maintaining trade-off between quality and cost is rather a difficult task for every private provider of health services. The reason is very obvious. When the providers want to enhance the quality of their health services naturally the cost goes up and the vice-versa.

Table 5.13 : The Problem of the Providers — Private Hospital Sector

1.	The high rate of staff turnover.	62.15	I
2.	The presence of stiff competition	57.30	II
3.	The complaining and agitating attitude of the patients	50.74	III
4.	The problem of maintaining trade [illegible]	[illegible]	[illegible]
5.	The easy availability of alternative medical treatments.	44.72	V

Source: Primary Data

Table 5.13 clearly exhibits the problems that are being encountered by providers of the private health sector. It is inferred from the table that the problem of 'the high rate of staff turnover' is ranked first with the highest mean score of 62.15 and followed by 'the presence of stiff competition' with a mean score 57.30. The problem titled 'the complaining and agitating attitude of the patients' is ranked third with the mean score of 50.74, 'the problem of maintaining trade-off between quality and cost' comes fourth with a mean score of 46.51 and the problem of 'easy availability of alternative medical treatments' stands last. Hence, it has the least mean score of 44.72.

Problems Encountered by the Providers of Public Health Sector

As every coin has two sides, the providers of public health sector have their own problems which may be different from the problems of the providers of private health sector. The following are the some of the major identified problems that have been encountered by the doctors of Government hospitals: Political interference, ineffective administration, inadequate manpower, poor maintenance of equipment and lack of doctors' commitment due to meager salary.

Political interference : The involvement of politicians in the conduct of Government hospitals is very much explicit. Most of the doctors of Government hospitals consider this interference of politicians into the affairs and administration of Government hospitals as an important problem. They consider this political inference as a stumbling block in the process of delivering quality health service to the public.

Ineffective administration : Effective administration always paves better way for the efficient and effective operation of delivering quality health service to the needy while ineffective administration does negatively affect the performance and the progress of the personnel of any organisation including public health organisations.

Inadequate manpower: Inadequate manpower has been considered as an important problem with regard to Government hospitals. Manpower includes physicians, doctors, nurses, sub-staff and the like. Due to inadequate manpower in Government hospitals, doctors find it great difficult to deliver quality health service to the public.

Poor maintenance of equipments : It is true that most of the Government hospitals do posses modern and sophisticated equipments. But, the agony is such hi-tech equipments are not properly and duly maintained. This poor maintenance of equipments eventually blocks the process of delivering quality health service to the public.

Lack of doctors' commitment due to meager salary : Doctors of Government hospitals too want handsome and decent pay packets. Though they feel happy about their medical profession and their Government service, they are not sufficiently happy with the pay that they presently receive. This meager salary ultimately leaves to lack of commitment on their part. Further, their lack of commitment towards this noble profession subsequently affects the quality of health service and also the quality of the nation.

Table 5.14 : Providers' Problem — Public Health Sector

1.	Ineffective administration	62.92	I
2.	Inadequate manpower	53.18	II
3.	Political interference	48.72	III
4.	Lack of commitment of doctors [illegible]	[illegible]	[illegible]
[illegible]	[illegible]	[illegible]	[illegible]

Source: Primary Data

Table 5.14 vividly reveals the problems that have been encountered by the providers of public health sector. It is evident from the table that of the five identified problems, ineffective administration has been considered as the first and foremost problem of the providers of Government hospitals with the highest mean score of 62.92 followed by 'inadequate manpower' with the mean score of 53.18. The problem of political interference is given third rank with a mean score of 48.72 and the fourth rank is given to the problem 'lack of commitment of doctors due to meager pay' with a mean score of 46.39. The fifth rank is given to the problem called 'poor maintenance of equipment' which has the least mean score of 43.21.

SUMMARY

This chapter aims at analysing the cost and return of providing healthcare services by the private hospitals and also studying the problems that have been encountered by the providers of both private healthcare service as well as the public healthcare service. In analysing the cost and return of hospital services, the cost per patient day and the P/V ratio have been arrived at by using the relevant formulae. The problems encountered by the doctors of both the private and the Government hospitals have been analysed and it was found out that of the five identified problems, the problem of 'high rate of staff turnover' is ranked as the first and foremost problem by the doctors of the private hospitals while the problem called 'ineffective administration' is ranked as the first and foremost problem by the doctors of the Government hospitals.

REFERENCES

1. Jha, S.M., 2007. *Hospital Management,* Himalaya Publishing House, Mumbai, p. 360.
2. Jain, S.P. and Narang, K.L., 2000. Hospital Costing, *Advanced Cost Accounting,* Kalyani Publishers, New Delhi, pp. 490-492.

CHAPTER 6

Summary of Findings, Suggestions and Conclusion

INTRODUCTION

This study has been undertaken with the following specific objectives: to study the profile of the health services provided in Kanyakumari district, to assess the socio-economic conditions of the patient respondents in the study area, to analyse the decision-making factors in the marketing of healthcare services, to asses the attitude of the patients towards marketing of hospital services, to assess the cost of hospital services and to analyse the costs and returns of the private healthcare providers, to assess and analyse the problems faced by the patients as well as the providers of the hospital services and to offer suitable suggestions to overcome the problems.

The study was primarily based on primary data — nevertheless, secondary data have also been used. The required primary data were collected from the sample patients and the providers of health services through the two specifically structured interview schedules. The collected primary data were duly analysed with the help of statistical tools like chi-square test, ANOVA, Garrett's ranking technique, factor anlaysis, discriminant analysis, cost and benefit analysis, and percentage analysis and inferences were drawn accordingly. This part of the study includes a summary of the major findings of the study, the suggestions and the conclusion.

SUMMARY OF FINDINGS

The following is the summary of the major findings of the study:

The Profile of Health Services Provided in Kanyakumari District

1. The healthcare system in Kanyakumari district comprises the Government and private sector health care institutions. The district has a good network of the Government hospitals (12), Primary Health Centres (PHCs — 31) and Health Sub-Centres (HSC—267) providing modern method of medical treatment to the patients.
2. The population covered by a HSC is 5,085 in India while it is 6,231 in Kanyakumari district. And, the population covered by a PHC is 31,954 in India while it is 53,870 in Kanyakumari district. These figures show inadequacy of the functioning of the public healthcare institutions in the study area.
3. The population per hospital bed ratio in Kanyakumari district is 1,185 as against 1,189 in the rest of Tamil Nadu. And, the population per doctor in Kanyakumari is 5,779 as against 6,240 per doctor in the rest of Tamil Nadu. Though the Government fund allotted to healthcare sector had always been in proportion to the population of the region, Kanyakumari district stands in a better position when compared with the rest of the districts of Tamil Nadu as regards the population per hospital bed ratio and population per doctor ratio.
4. The private sector health services in the district ranges from those provided by the large corporate hospitals, smaller hospitals/nursing homes, clinics/dispensaries run by qualified personnel. The hospitals and hospital beds in the private sector are skewed towards urban areas. The private healthcare sector includes 295 hospitals providing varied health services inclusive of

nursing homes and clinics. In Kanyakumari district, there are more than 750 private healthcare professionals.

The Socio-economic Profile of Patient Respondents and Their Use of Government or Private Hospitals

1. It is inferred that whatever age group the respondents may belong to, *there was no noticeable change* among the respondents in availing services either from Government hospitals or from private hospitals.
2. It is inferred from the study that while more number of male respondents (57.44 per cent) availed health services from the Government hospitals more number of female respondents (56.60 per cent) availed health services from the private hospitals.
3. It is inferred that when the marital status of the respondents shifted from unmarried to married they utilized the Government hospital services more frequently.
4. It is inferred from the study that the patients whose level of *literacy was high* (83.87 per cent), utilized the *private hospitals* more and the patients whose level of *literacy was low* (65.21 per cent), utilized the *Government hospital* services more.
5. It is inferred that where the respondents whose occupational status was *low* utilized the *Government* hospital services more and the respondents whose occupational status was *high* utilized the *private hospital* services more frequently.
6. It is inferred that the respondents whose *monthly income was high,* utilized the *private hospital services more* and the respondents whose *monthly income was less,* utilized the *Government hospital services more frequently.*
7. It is inferred from the study that when the size of the family of the respondents was *large,* they utilized the *Government* hospitals more and when the size of the family was *small,* they utilized the *private* hospital services more.

8. It is inferred that the respondents whose residential was *rural* (61.67 per cent), utilized the *Government hospital* services more and the respondents whose residential status was *urban* (67.5 per cent), utilized the *private hospital* services more frequently.

Factors Motivating the Decision-making in Choosing the Government/the Private Hospitals

1. It was found out that first of all *'cost of health services'* provides the maximum insights of buying decision of the patients of the Government hospitals in the study area. It is a very important factor because the respondents prefer to avail health services from the Government hospitals at a cheaper cost if not cost free. Secondly, patients choose to avail health services from the Government hospitals because of the peripheral services available in the Government hospitals. Thirdly, patients are encouraged to avail core health services provided by the Government hospitals.
2. It was also found out that factors like *'pre-consultancy services'* and *'quality of health services'* were also play an important role in decision making, in order to avail health services from the Government hospitals.
3. It could be inferred that the selection decision behaviour of the patients of the Government hospitals was significantly influenced by the *'quality of health services'*. One per cent increase in the "quality of health services", keeping all other factors constant will show an increase by choosing of the Government hospitals by decision-making behaviour by 0.1142 per cent from its mean level.
4. It was found out that *'Quality of health services'* provides the maximum insights of selection decision of the private hospitals in the study area and it is a very important factor because the respondents prefer to avail health services of high quality. To improve this situation, private providers of health services should give more

importance on the attributes concerning 'quality of health services'. Secondly, patients choose the private hospitals to avail health services if they are satisfied with the core services provided by the hospitals. Thirdly, patients are encouraged to avail health services from private hospitals if the hospitals provide adequate pre-consultancy services and sufficient peripheral services.

5. The factors *'familiarity', 'location of the hospital'* and 'cost of health services' were also important in making a decision as to selecting the private hospitals.
6. The selection decision bahaviour of the patients of the private hospitals was also influenced by the *'cost of health service'*. The co-efficient of cost was -0.0962 which was significant at one per cent level. This shows that *one per cent decrease in the cost* of the health service of the private hospitals would increase the selection decision by 0.0952 per cent from its mean level.

Discriminant Variables Leading to Selection Decision

1. It is inferred from the study that the important discriminant variables leading to selection decision among the patients of the Government maternity and paediatric and the private maternity and paediatric hospitals are the *cost of health services, the core services* and *the quality of services.*
2. It is inferred from the study that the important discriminant variables leading to selection decision among the patients of the Government orthopaedic and general medicine and the private orthopaedic and general medicine hospitals are *familiarity, core services* and *cost of health services.*

The Attitude of the Patients Towards Marketing of Hospital Services

1. It is observed that the patients of the Government hospitals have poor attitude towards location of the

hospitals while there is a prevalence of better attitude among the patients in the private maternity and paediatric hospitals as well as the private orthopaedic and general medicine hospitals.

2. The study reveals that there is an existence of poor attitude towards pre-consultancy services among the patients of the Government hospitals and better attitude among the patients of the private hospitals.
3. It is found that the *patients of the private hospitals* have *better attitude* towards *core services* when compared to the attitude of the patients of the Government hospitals.
4. It is inferred from the study that although by and large the patients of the private hospitals have better attitude towards the maximum factors on peripheral services, in the case of certain factors like 'ambulance service' and 'canteen facility the patients of the Government hospitals have greater positive attitude when compared to the attitude of the patients of the private hospitals.
5. The study reveals that more or less the patients of both the healthcare sectors namely the public and the private have the same level of attitude towards 'transparency of hospitals'.
6. The study reveals that there exists a *poor attitude* among the patients of the *Government hospitals* as regards the *quality of services* when compared with the attitude of the patients of the private hospitals.
7. As regards hygienic conditions, the study reveals that the patients of the Government hospitals have poor attitude and there exists a better attitude among the patients of the private hospitals.
8. It has been observed that there is a lower level of Hospitality Index (HI) of the Government hospital patients when compared to the HI of the patients of the private hospitals.
9. The study reveals that the poor attitude towards physical evidences of health services is found among

the patients of the Government hospitals and a better attitude towards physical evidences of health services is found among the patients of the private hospitals.

10. It is found that the poor attitude towards innovativeness is found among the patients of the Government hospitals and a *better attitude among the patients of the private hospitals.*
11. The study reveals that the poor attitude towards familiarity is found among the patients of the private hospitals and a better attitude among the patients of the Government hospitals.

Findings on Testing of Hypotheses

1. It is found that *there is no significant relationship* between the age group and the level of attitude of the sample respondents towards the services provided by the hospitals in Kanyakumari district.
2. It is found that *there exists no significant relationship* between the gender and the level of attitude of the sample respondents towards the services provided by the hospitals in Kanyakumari district.
3. It is found that *there exists significant relationship* between the literacy level and the level of attitude of the sample respondents towards the services provided by the hospitals in Kanyakumari district.
4. It is found that *there exists significant relationship* between occupational status and the level of attitude of the sample respondents towards the services provided by the hospitals in Kanyakumari district.
5. It is found that *there exists no significant relationship* between the marital status and the level of attitude of the sample respondents towards the services provided by the hospitals in Kanyakumari district.
6. It is found that *there exists significant relationship* between family income and the level of attitude of the sample

respondents towards the services provided by the hospitals in Kanyakumari district.

7. It is found that *there exists significant relationship* between the number of members in the family — that is size of the family and the level of attitude of the sample respondents towards the services provided by the hospitals in Kanyakumari district.
8. It is found that *there exists significant relationship* between the area of residence and the level of attitude of the sample respondents towards the services provided by the hospitals in Kanyakumari district.

The Profile of the Sample Provider Respondents

1. It is inferred from the study that the majority of 59 per cent of the sample hospitals have more than 10 years of service in providing health services. However, it is also inferred that the majority of the sample private hospitals (52 per cent) have a shorter length of service of below 5 years and 5-10 years.
2. It is inferred that the sample private hospitals have more number of beds than those of the sample public sector hospitals.
3. It is inferred that the majority of the sample public sector health institutions (60 per cent) are in the form of PHCs and most of the sample private sector health institutions (80 per cent) are in the form of hospitals.
4. It is found that there is non-existence of marketing department as such in the entire sample public sector hospitals. But the marketing department exists only in four of the total sample private hospitals.
5. It is observed that the orthopaedic private hospitals had invested more than that of the private maternity, paediatric and general medicine hospitals.

The Costs and Returns Analysis of the Providers of Private Health Services

1. It is inferred that the *share of the variable cost* to the total costs (65.10 per cent) is *greater* than that of the share of fixed costs (34.90 per cent) to the total costs in providing private maternity services.
2. It is found that while the *cost per patient day* of maternity health service amounts to Rs. 1767.14 the profit per patient day is Rs. 669.98. Further, the profit volume ratio is *52.79 per cent.*
3. It is revealed in the study that the share of the variable costs to the total costs for providing private paediatric service is (55.02 per cent) *higher* than the share of fixed costs (44.98 per cent) to the total costs.
4. It is found that the *cost per patient day* of providing private paediatric service is Rs. 433.21 and the *profit per patient day* amounts to Rs. 175.13. It is also inferred that the profit volume ratio is *60.82 per cent.*
5. In the case of providing private orthopaedic health services, the share of the total annual *variable costs* towards the total annual costs *(77.18 per cent)* is much greater than that of the share of the total fixed costs (22.82 per cent).
6. It is also found that while the cost per patient day of providing private orthopaedic service amounts to Rs. 4,244.96 the *profit per patient day* is Rs. 1080.95. Further it is inferred that the profit volume ratio is *38.48 per cent.*

The Problems Faced by Patient Respondents

1. It is inferred from the study that out of the five identified problems, the problem of *'high fees'* is ranked as the first and foremost problem by the patients of the private hospitals with the highest mean score of 54.32 followed by the *'problem of discrimination in providing quality services'* with a mean score of 49.28. The problem

'poor pre-consultancy services' is ranked third with the mean score of 47.15 followed by 'discrimination in fixing fees' with a mean score of 42.93 and the last rank is given to *'long waiting time'* with the least mean score of 40.18.

2. It is inferred from the study that out of the five identified problems, the problem of *'no personal attention'* is ranked first by the patients of the Government hospitals with the highest mean score 58.37 followed by *'poor quality of service'* with a mean score of 55.11. The problem of 'poor hygienic conditions' has been ranked third with a mean score of 51.17 followed by *'inadequate staff for emergency'* with a mean score 44.08. The problem called 'tips / money demanded by sub-staff' has been ranked the last with the least mean score of 41.30.

The Problems Encountered by the Providers of Health Services

1. It is inferred from the study that the problem of *'high rate of staff turnover'* is ranked first by the providers of private health services with the highest mean score of 62.15 and followed by *'presence of stiff competition'* with a mean score 57.30. The problem titled 'patient complaining and agitating attitude' is ranked third with the mean score of 50.74 by the providers of private health services and the fourth rank is given to the *'problem of maintaining trade-off between quality and cost'* and the last rank is given to the problem called 'easy availability of alternative medical treatments'. Hence, it has the least mean score of 44.72.
2. It is evident from the study that out of the five identified problems, *ineffective administration* has been considered as the first and foremost problem of the providers of the Government hospitals with the highest mean score of 62.92 followed by *'inadequate manpower'* with the mean score of 53.18. The problem of political interference is given the third rank with a mean score of 48.72 and the

fourth rank is given to the problem 'lack of commitment of doctors due to meager pay' with a mean score of 46.39. The fifth rank is given to the problem called *'poor maintenance of equipment'* which has the least mean score of 43.21.

SUGGESTIONS

Based on the study, the following suggestions are offered:

1. It is suggested that in order to provide adequate public healthcare services in the study area, the concerned and competent Governmental authorities have to look into this issue and do the needful at the earliest.
2. The study reveals that by and large the patients of the Government hospitals have poor attitude towards certain aspects of the hospital marketing such as pre-consultancy services, core services, quality of health services, hygienic conditions, physical evidences of health services and innovativeness in medical treatment. Hence, appropriate actions should be taken at the earliest to provide quality health services by the public sector and thereby serve the needy in the best possible way.
3. Since the problem of *'high fees'* has been ranked first by the patients of the private hospitals it is suggested that despite the incurrence of high costs in delivering quality health services, the providers are expected to find out some means such as controlling both variable and fixed costs, *downsizing the margin* to lowering the fee eventually. So also it is suggested not to show any kind of discrimination to the patients in the process of providing quality service to them. Further, the private hospitals in general have to strengthen the system of pre-consultancy services by evolving and implementing a fool-proof token system, and maintaining suitable consulting hours so as to satisfy the patients and by and large to retain them for quite a long period.

4. The patients of the Government hospitals consider the problem *'No personal attention'* as the first and foremost problem. Hence, the providers of public health services are reminded of the need and the importance of accommodating the patients politely and patiently. Further, the Governmental authorities have to make necessary arrangements and assure that quality health services are delivered in Government hospitals. It is also suggested to put in enough efforts to make sure the premises of the public sector health establishments namely the Government hospitals, PHCs and HSCs have better hygienic conditions.
5. As it is found out in the study that although the private orthopaedic hospitals have invested heavily than that of its other two counterparts it has the least p/v ratio. Hence, *evolving and executing an effective cost control system* becomes the need of the hour. Therefore, it is suggested to the providers of private orthopaedic services that evolve and execute an effective cost control system to control the variable costs in general and the costs of medicine in specific so as to cut down their total costs and eventually to enhance the profit-volume ratio.
6. Since a *high rate of staff turnover* has been experienced as the first and foremost problem of the providers of the private health sector, it is suggested to orient the staff in such a way that they are loyal to their hospital authorities. Further, the providers are also expected to sensitize the financial and psychological needs of their personnel so as to retain if not reduce the rate of staff turnover and thereby to enhance the performance of the private healthcare institutions. And, the providers of the private healthcare services are excepted to orient and educate their patients about the complex nature of providing healthcare services so that their attitude of complaining and agitating is no more encouraged.

7. As it is evident from the study that *ineffective administration* has been considered as the first and the foremost problem of the providers of the Government hospitals, the Government of India, the state of Tamil Nadu and the district administration have to seriously consider this and gear up activities which are essential for the effective administration of the establishments of public health sector namely the Government hospitals, the PHCs and the HSCs. Further, the Government and the public health department are to see that adequate manpower is employed in the Government hospitals, the PHCs and the HSCs. And, it is also suggested that as far as possible it should be seen that there is no unnecessary political interference which hinders the smooth provisioning of health services to the public.

CONCLUSION

The researcher feels that the study has served the purposes for which it was carried out. As the study is a novel one, a humble and a maiden attempt has been made by the researcher to explore the avenues as to fulfil the objectives of the study. Sincere efforts have been made by the researcher to study the chosen problem of marketing of hospital services in the study area. Despite the inherent and inevitable limitations of the study, all the specified objectives have been genuinely arrived at. As health matters a lot to every individual of a nation and as health has been considered as an important determinant of a nation's Human Development Index (HDI), the researcher gets a sense of satisfaction in completing this tiny research endeavour. The study is of its first kind in exploring the costs and returns analysis of the providers of the private health sector. With the help of the first hand information that are supplied by the providers as to the costs incurred in and the revenues generated by delivering health services by the providers of the private hospitals, it is possible to arrive at the costs and the returns associated with marketing of hospital services. The study gives a vivid picture of the socio-economic profile of the sample patient respondents and their pattern of availing treatment from the Government hospitals and / or the private hospitals. The factors that are responsible for choosing either a Government hospital or a private hospital are duly and analytically presented in the study. Above all, the attitude of the patients towards marketing of hospital services has been exhaustively presented. The researcher hopes that the findings of the study would be of great help for both the patients and the providers of both the private as well as the Government hospitals. The researcher strongly believes that if the suggestions that are offered in the study are duly considered and subsequently if necessary actions are taken by the officials concerned and also by the providers of the health services, prompt delivery of the promised quality health services could be assured. Despite the above mentioned fruits of this research endeavour, the researcher is not fully contented with the study due to its own inherent and inevitable limitations. The researcher hopes very strongly that still there is an ample scope for further research on different dynamics and dimensions of hospital marketing.

Areas of and Scope for Further Research

Based on the findings of the present study, the following issues have been identified for further research:

1. Patients' perceptions and preferences towards private hospitals.
2. Healthcare Industry in India in the post liberalization era.
3. The perceptions and preferences of patients towards allopathic medical treatment over the other alternative medical treatments.
4. Effective public health system — A source of empowering the underprivileged.

5. Slum dwellers' accessibility towards health services — An empirical study in Tamil Nadu.
6. A descriptive study on Healthcare Industry in Tamil Nadu.
7. Origin and growth of medical tourism in India with particular reference to Chennai, Tamil Nadu.

There are still more researchable areas to be addressed and genuine problems to be redressed in this field of healthcare industry. The researcher is confident that this small piece of research work on professional service marketing in general and on healthcare marketing in specific will definitely kindle a keen interest in the minds of the budding and future researchers. On such an event, the researcher would feel proud and delighted. The researcher takes pride in concluding the study with his vision of *'constituting a wealthy India through healthy Indians'* by 2020 since health is wealth and good health confers on the citizens of a nation both freedom from illness and the ability to realise and actualise their potential and contribute to the nation's well-being.

Bibliography

Books

Arunkumar, Meenakshi, N., 2006. Marketing Management Comprehensive Text, Best Practices, Corporate Insights, Vikas Publishing House Pvt. Ltd. First Edition, New Delhi.

Balaji, B., 2006. Services Marketing and Management, Second Revised Edition, S. Chand Company Ltd. New Delhi.

Biplab S. Bose, 2007. Marketing Management, First Edition, Himalaya Publishing House, Mumbai.

Chunawalla, S.A., 2005. Commentary on Consumer Behaviour, Himalaya Publishing House, Second Revised Edition, Delhi.

George Joseph, John Desrochers, Mariamma Kalathil, 1978. Health Care in India, Centre for Social Action, Bangalore.

Govind Aptc, 2004. Service Marketing, Oxford University Press, New Delhi.

Harish V. Verma, 2002. Services Marketing Text and Cases, Pearson Eduaction, Delhi.

Henry E., Garrett and Woodworth, 1969. Statistics in Psychology and Education, Vikas Fetter and Sciences Private Ltd., Bombay.

Jain, S.P. and Narang, K.L., 2000. Hospital Costing, Advanced Cost Accounting, Kalyani Publishers, New Delhi.

Jeggi, 1979. History of Science, Technology and Medicine in India, Western Medicine in India, Atma Ram & Sons, Delhi.

Jha, S.M. 2007. Hospital Management, Himalaya Publishing House, Mumbai.

Jha, S.M., 2000. Service Marketing, Millennium edition. Himalaya Publishing House, Mumbai.

John Frain, 1986. The Principles and Practice of Marketing, Pitman Publishing Limited, London.

John Wilmshurst, 2004. The Fundamentals and Practice of Marketing, Third Edition, Viva Books Private Limited, New Delhi.

Karunakaran, 2007. Marketing Management (Text and Cases in Indian Context) Himalaya Publishing House, New Delhi.

Kenneth E. Clow, David L. Kurtz, 2003. Services Marketing: Operation, Management and Strategy, Second Edition, Biztantra, An Imprint of Dreamtech Press, New Delhi.

Kothari, C.R., 2006. Research Methodology—Methods and Techniques, New Age International Private Limited Publishers, New Delhi.

Leon G. Schiffman, Leslie Lazar Kanum, 2008. Consumer Behaviour, Ninth Edition, Pearson Education, Delhi.

Mamoria, C.B., Suri, R.K., Satish Mamoria, 1999. Marketing Management, Kitab Mahal, New Delhi.

Micheal J. Etzel, Bruce J. Walker, William J. Stanton, Ajay Pandit, 2006. Marketing, 13th Edition, Tata McGraw-Hill Publishing Company Limited, New Delhi.

Pat Weymes, 1990. How to Perfect Your Selling Skills, Wheeler Publishing, New Delhi.

Paul Peter, J., Jerry C. Olson, 2005. Consumer Behaviour and Marketing Strategy, Seventh Edition, New Delhi.

Philip Kotler and Paul N. Bloom, 1992. Marketing Professional Services, Prentice Hall Inc., Englewood Cliffs, New Jersey.

Philip Kotler, Gary Arumstrong, 2005. Principles of Marketing, Eleventh Edition, Prentice-Hall of India Private Limited, New Delhi.

Philip Kotler, Kevin Lane Keller, 2005. Marketing Management, Twelth Edition, Prentice-Hall of India Private Limited, New Delhi.

Rajendra Nargundkar, 2006. Services Marketing Text and Cases, Second Edition, Tata McGraw-Hill Publishing Company Limited, New Delhi.

Raju, M.S., Dominique Xardel, 2006. Marketing Management International Perspectives, Vijay Nicole Imprints Private Limited, Chennai.

Rama Mohana Rao, K., 2005. Services Marketing, Pearson Education, Delhi.

Ramaswamy, V.S., Namakumar, S., 2006. Marketing Management Planning, Implementing and Control — Global Perspective Indian Context Third Edition, Macmillan India Ltd. Delhi.

Rampal, M.K., Gupta, S.C. 2000. Services Marketing - Concepts, Applications and Cases, Galgotia Publishing Company, New Delhi.

Ravi Shankar, 2006. Services Marketing the Indian Perspective Text and Readings, Excel Books, New Delhi.

Rustom S. Davar, Sohrab R. Davar and Nulsi R. Davar, 1982. Modern Marketing Management in the Indian Context, Sixth Edition, Progressive Corporation Private Limited, Bombay.

Sherlekar, S.A., 2002. Marketing Management (Integrated Manaement Approach Under Current Market Driven and Competitive Global Marketing), Himalaya Publishing House, Delhi.

Sherleker, S.A., Vivendra Sharad Sherlekar, 2002. Global Marketing Management (Under Value-based Integrated Customised Approach), Mumbai.

Sontakki, C.N., Deshpande, R.G., 1979. Marketing, Salesmanship and Advertising , Kalyani Publishers, New Delhi.

Srinivasan, A.V. 2000. Managing a Modern Hospital, Response Books, New Delhi.

Srivastava, K.K., Sujatha Khandal, 2002. Consumer Behaviour in Indian Context, Galgotia Publishing Company, New Delhi.

Valarie A. Zeithamal, Mary Jo Bitner, 2003. Services Marketing - Integrating Customer Focus Across the Firm, Tata McGraw-Hill Publishing Company Limited, New Delhi.

Vasanti Venugopal, Ragu, V.N., 2007. Service Marketing, Hiamalya Publishing House, Delhi.

Verneker, S.S., Sandeep Goel, Bhardwaj, B.R., 2005. Marketing of Services - Strategies for Growth, Deep and Deep Publications Pvt. Ltd. New Delhi.

Warren K. Keegan, 2005. Global Marketing Management, Seventh Edition, Pearson Education, Delhi.

William J. Stanton, Charles Futrell, 1987. Fundamental of Marketing, Tata McGraw, Hill Book Company, Eight Edition, New Delhi, 1987.

Yogendra Singh, Mamta Pandey, 2004, International Business and Marketing Management, First Edition, A.I.T.B.S. Publishers and Distributors, Delhi.

Theses

Babitha, R., 2007. A Descriptive Study of Healthcare Industry in Kanyakumari District, Research Centre in Commerce, Manonmaniam Sundaranar University, Tirunelveli.

Deepa Sankar, 2001. Access to and Utilisation of Healthcare Sector in Kerala: Patterms and Determinants, Centre for Development Studies, Trivandrum.

Mohan, C.K. 1973, Production, Marketing and Price Behaviour of Pepper in Vazhoor Block of Kerala State, Tamil Nadu Agricultural University, Coimbatore.

Panneerselvem, A., 1998. Marketing of Professional Services with particular reference to Hospitals in Madras, Tamil Nadu, Bharathidhasan University, Trichy.

Journals, Magazines and Newspapers

Angela, M. Rushton and David J. Carson, 1985. The Marketing of Services: Managing the intangibles, *European Journal of Marketing,* Vol. 19.

Babu, T.D., Jayabal, G., "Healthcare in India: Opportunities and Challenges", *Business and Economic Facts for You,* April 2004, Vol. 24, No. 7.

Balasubramanian, B., 2008. English Language Adeptness and Health Literacy, *The Journal of English Language Teaching (India),* Vol. XLVI.

Bharati Rawla, The Health Proposition, *The Economic Times,* Wednesday 4th May, 1994.

Bhat Ramesh, 1999. Characteristics of Private Medical Practice in India: A Provider Perspective, *Health Policy and Planning,* Vol. 14.

Bunker, J.P., 2001. "The Role of Medical Care in Contributing to Health Improvement in Within Societies", *International Journal of Epidemiology,* Vol. 30.

Debabar Banerji, 2006. Labour Some of the Basic Principle of Distribution of Public Health Practice in India, *International Journal of Health Services*, Vol. 36.

Deogaonkar, Milind, 2004. Socio-economic Inequality and Its Effect on Healthcare Delivery in India: Inequality and Healthcare, *Electronic Journal of Sociology*.

Evert Gummesson, How Professional Services are Brought, *Journal of Marketing*, Vol. 15.

Gina B. Krishnan, Quality Care, Cover Story, The Check-ups, *Business World*, 15th July, 2005.

Horace E. Jonhs and Ronald Moser, H. 1988. How Consumers View Hospital Advertising, *Journal of Hospital Marketing*, Vol. 3.

Jugand, 2008. Cover Feature, Health Care, *The Week*, August 31.

Mittal, M.P. and Saxena, P.P., 1975. A Mathematical Expressions for Cost and Analysis of Farm Equipments" – *Indian Journal of Agricultural Economics*, Vol. 29, No. 1.

Paul F. Clark, 2006. The Globalization of the labour Market for Health Care Professionals, *International Labour Review*, Vol. 145.

Priya Deshpande, 2006. Service Quality Perspective and Satisfaction in Health Care Systems – A Study of Select Hospitals in Hyderabad, *Indian Journal of Marketing*, Vol. 37.

Rajan Modhok, Quality of Hospital Service, *Journal of Public Health*, Vol. 14.

Rama Jeyasundar, 2008. Ancient vs. New Approach to Health, *Kisan World*, Vol. 35

Seema Joshi, 2006. From Conventional to New Services, The *Indian Journal of Labour Economics*, Vol. 49.

Singh D.R. Sunaina, 2005. Management of Health Care Services Sector — A Study on Primary Health Centres, *Indian Journal of Marketing*, Vol. 12.

Sumit Ghoshal, Pre-empting Illness, Executive Health Survey, *Business India*, September 7, 2008.

Varatharajan, D., 2006. India's Human Development: Gaps and Prospects, *Health and Population – Perspectives and Issues*, Vol. 29.

WHO, 1978, *National Academy of Psychology, India*, Vol. 51.

The Hindu, India's National Newspaper, November 14, 2008

The Hindu, India's National Newspaper, November 19, 2008

Reports, Research Papers, Hand Books, Manuals and Proceedings

State Primary Census Abstract of Total Population, *Census,* 2001.

Indian Medical Association (Tamil Nadu) *Directory,* 2006.

Department of Economics and Statistics — Kanyakumari District, *District Statistical Hand Book,* 2007.

"Studies on the Economics of Farm Management in Tanjore, *Report for the Year 1969-70",* Directorate of Economics and Statistics, Ministry of Agriculture and Irrigation, Government of India, New Delhi, 1974.

Studies on Economics of Management in Coimbatore District, Tamil Nadu, *Directorate of Economics and Statistics,* 1971-72, New Delhi.

Jezer Jebanesan, Babita, A Swot Analysis of the Health Care Industry in Kanyakumari District, *Proceedings: Fourth Multi-disciplinary National Seminar,* SRF-2007.

Daniel, R.R., "Citizens" Report on the State of Development and Enviornment in Kanyakumari District, *South Vision,* Chennai.

Muraleedharan, Characteristics and Structure of Private Hospital Sector in Urban India: A study of Madras City, *Small Applied Area Research Paper.*

Websites

www.insead.edu

www.mohfw.nic.in

www.tn.gov.in

www.ibef.org

www.expressheatlhcaremanagement.com

www.healthcareindustryindia.com

www.tnhealth.org

en.wikipedia.org

www.hinduonnet.com

www.hospimedia-india.com

Index

❑❑❑